F.A.Q.

Frequently Asked Questions about techniques used for painting cars and motorcycles

Juan Layos
Juan de Dios Catena

www.lycmodelers.com

ANDREA
PRESS

CREDITS

Original idea, models, texts and photographs by
Juan Layos and Juan de Dios Catena.

www.lycmodelers.com

Editorial Director:
Javier Huerta

Published by:
ANDREA PRESS
C/ Talleres, 21
Pol. Ind. de Alpedrete
28430 Alpedrete (Madrid)
Tel: 91 857 00 08
Fax: 91 857 00 48
www.andrea-miniatures.com
andrea@andrea-miniatures.com

Printed by
ATIG (Spain)

ISBN: 978-84-96658-08-0

This book was written between
August 2006 and August 2007.

This work is dedicated to our parents, whose
patience was tested and who, nevertheless, never
complained about the inconvenience and
difficulties that were encountered as we mastered
our hobby.

● *INTRODUCTION*

1.THE BOOK

1.1 Who is this book aimed at?

In this book, you will discover a compendium of knowledge and wisdom gathered through the years by way of our own trial and error experiences, other helpful modellers, publications, competitions, and many other sources. Because of this wealth of gathered knowledge, Andrea Press approached us to create a work of this kind, a project that was finally shaped into a written book covering techniques and knowledge on 'civil modelling', as it is known in the modelling argot, that is specifically aimed to reach anybody with a love of building model cars, whether they be novice or skilled modeller. The goal was to create a didactical diffusion of this modelling specialty from our own personal point of view to encourage other modellers how to fully enjoy this wonderful field in the hobby.

Unlike other modelling specialities, a number of unique techniques are used to render a realistic, clean and highly detailed finish, especially on bodywork, that must, as much as possible, be perfect.

Often, in competitions and specialized magazines, we are not given as much credit as other modellers who make, say, tanks, planes, figures, etc. Fortunately, the market supplies us with much fine material to improve our models. There is a constant stream of new, exciting and exclusive models released by various manufacturers that, in turn, has attracted more and more modellers into the art of building cars and motorcycles. Now and then, even modellers who usually concentrate on other fields of modelling have been attracted to try this type of models with very satisfactory results.

However, it should never be forgotten that this is our hobby, our passion. It is something we enjoy doing, it releases us from daily routine and relaxes us, and gives us a sense of satisfaction, not problems.

The end result doesn't really matter if, when we consider a completed model, has the time it has taken been one of enjoyment, regardless of the quality obtained or the effort involved. Of course, it is always possible to make things difficult by selecting a very complex model or –on the contrary- just to choose another, very simple one just to kill time.

We would never recommend that you take on 'more than you can chew', as the saying goes. If you do, our experience tells us that it is best to lay it aside until such time as you have gained enough experience and are skilled enough to succeed and, meanwhile, start another, simpler project. By proceeding deeper than your skill allows is usually a shortcut to abandoning the hobby...and that would be a shame

Another interesting topic for modellers is competitions. Obviously, we all like our work to be recognized and to collect that sought-after award. However, it is now widely known that, quite often, competitions are not always a fair judgement and judges' criteria may not always be coincidental with our hopes. This fact makes some modellers opt out of the hobby out of desperation and frustration. Of course, competitions should not be used just to collect awards. On the contrary, they should be viewed as a means of allowing us to share our interests and concerns with other modellers and to compete with others in a healthy, sporting way.

1.2 Who are we?

We got to know each other quite a long time ago thanks to a common friend, Emiliano López Cano. He introduced us because he was aware of our common interest in the same area of modelling. However, it is now approximately eight years since destiny caused us to work in the same building and that, every now and again, we met aboard the train taking us home in the evening. Naturally, conversation soon drifted to our shared passion: models. How could it be any other way! This resulted in the foundation of a lasting relationship of mutual support and contribution that has undoubtedly allowed us to evolve much faster than if we had been working independently. There have never been any secrets between us, and we were both always glad to share any new discovery. This helped us to go deeper into the hobby and improvement became noticeable almost from the first day. Soon, we began to gain awards at competitions and were asked to contribute articles for specialist magazines, including the Spanish Euromodelismo, and even to run courses on the subject.

In the following pages, we have set out to encourage all of you to share your skills with others, thereby contributing to the health and development of our hobby that, at times, is an excellent means of diminishing personal problems and putting everything into perspective.

1.3 Remarks

As stated earlier, this book has been composed with a didactical aim. Quite obviously, all the explained techniques are not necessarily the best or the only ones, but simply… our own. In a way, we felt compelled to share them in the hope they might prove useful to other modellers.

The express mention of particular manufacturers or brands has been intentionally avoided and, by no means do we suggest that the ones used here are the best or, indeed, the most suitable. Each modeller must find his/her own way to feel comfortable with the result through the use of their own favourite products. We have set out to show just one among many possibilities. Take it as a point of departure.

We have attempted to include all the more popular specialities to explain the different techniques and processes: a GP motorcycle; a rally car from the World Rally Championship; a typical classic from Le Mans (Toyota GT ONE); an Aston Martin DBR9 from the GT Championship; another from the same competition (Ferrari 550), and, finally, an example from F1. These last two in a smaller scale. We earnestly hope that all the models shown are representative enough to enable you to use the same techniques on any other vehicle.

1.4 Acknowledgements

After a year of work that, of necessity, had to be shared with our full-time working careers and family commitments, the book was finally completed. It has been an unforgettable experience and, at times, a bit too hard, although we are more than satisfied with the end result. We gave much in the way of enthusiasm and dedication but received much in the way of enjoyment as a reward. We earnestly hope you enjoy it too.

Finally, we would like to express our sincere thanks for the contributions of Loli Herráez Diaz-Crespo, Javier Catena and, especially, Guillermo Coll who constantly encouraged us and helped us to grow and evolve as modellers.

Juan Layos.

Juan de Dios Catena.

'Los Juanes'; so nicknamed by their modelling friends.

2. *THE WORKPLACE*

2.1 *How should the workplace look?*

In principle, there is no need for a large work area, although it is, of course, recommendable to have at one's disposal a private, permanent area to leave any work-in-progress without being obliged to clear up all the tools and parts after each modelling session. If you have such an area, you are able to take up modelling at any spare moment.

However, whatever space you have for your modelling, it must be kept tidy. At times, a little chaos is generated but it can be kept under control. Never let it get out of hand because this will eventually lead to desperation. When this point is arrived at, stop working and proceed to clear up the workbench.

**Note how basic tools are at hand
and stored in different containers;
all placed out of harms way.**

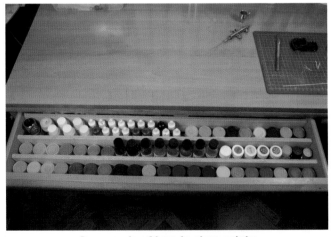

**An example of how to store paints:
special cubicles have been created
in a drawer using simple wooden strips.**

A large table is also not really needed. In fact, the work area could be just a corner of the table. Saying that, one does require some extra space for storing completed models, work-in-progress parts, other parts, tools, brushes and all the other necessary modelling equipment.

With regards to a modelling light, avoid, at all costs, a yellow tungsten one. Of course, if possible, it is better to work in daylight and facing a window that, incidentally, will also come in handy when dealing with paint or any other toxic product.

Make sure that all the reference material you need to complete a given project is kept close at hand.

Using a lamp as well as natural daylight. Even if working in daylight conditions, it is advisable to also have a lamp.

In this case, the reference material is close at hand but in a raised position to avoid books, photos etc, from being damaged by paints or solvents. The kit instructions can be pinned to a cork panel.

3. TOOLS

3.1 What basic tools should I have?

A varied selection of good quality tools will make a success of any proposed project. In fact, it is probably the best investment you can make. Obviously, a modicum of practice will be required to perfect some level of competence in their use. However, once mastered, a good tool will reward your investment with a greatly enhanced final result.

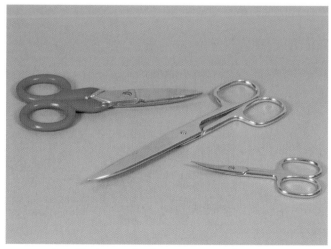

Specific types of scissors are used dependent on material or pattern.

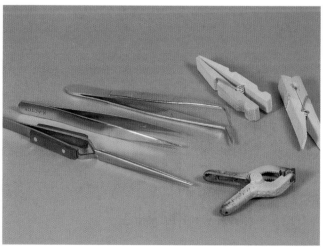

Tweezers are an indispensable item for assisting in the assembly of delicate parts and also for holding parts during painting.

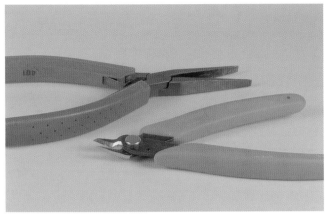

Pliers and side cutters. Different quality side cutters are used dependent on the hardness of the material to be cut. Careless use will damage the cutting edges.

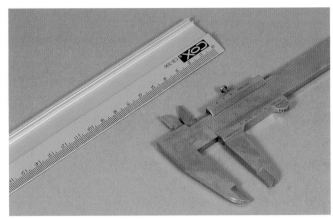

A steel rule or calipers are extremely useful for checking measurements to see that they comply with the scale measurements of the actual vehicle being modelled.

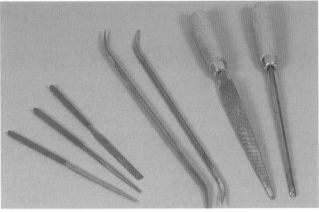

Files of different shape, grade and size.

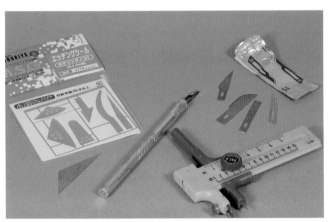

Precision screwdrivers.

Photo-etched and jewellers' saws, and a cutting compass.

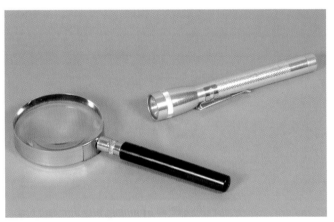

A magnifying glass and flash light are a 'must' for detecting any tiny flaws.

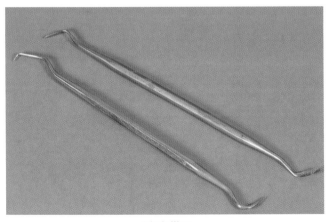

Modelling palettes.

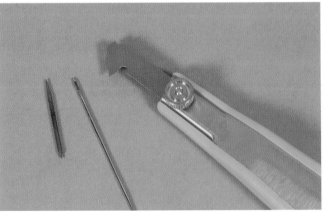

A sharp punch and a scriber are the most suitable for re-defining lines on bodywork.

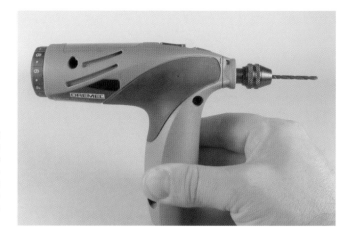

Mini-drills are extremely useful for drilling and milling. Both the speed and the drill-holder should be adjustable. Speed is important, especially when working with plastic, as too high a rate may cause it to melt.

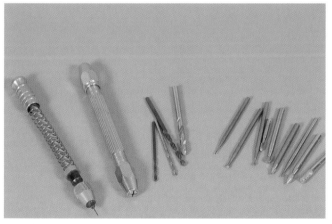

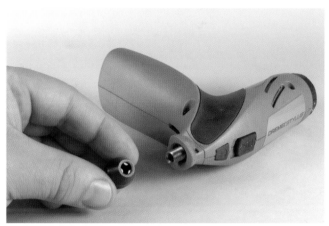

Hand drill holder, different sizes of milling bits and drill bits.

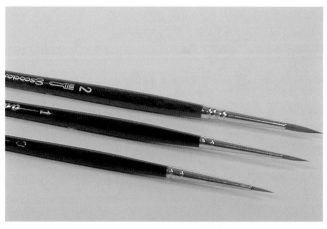

At least three, high quality brushes (preferably of Kolinsky sable) are required. The points should be carefully maintained as they are used for precision work.

Flat brushes for dry brushing
(see point 25).

Small flat brushes used only
for positioning decals.

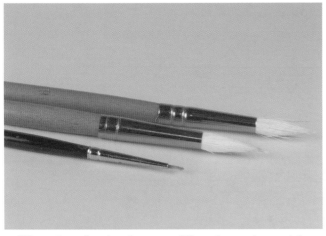

Old, or cheap brushes for many different uses, i.e. applying putty, glue, and reproducing textures, etc.

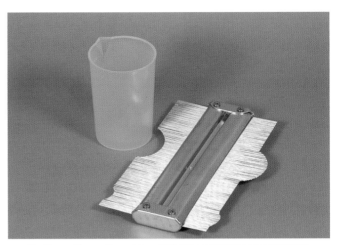

A silhouette pattern is useful for comparing geometries.

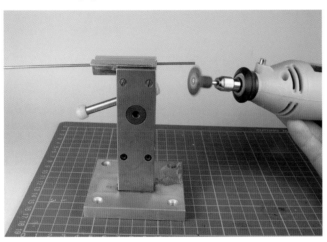

Stand.

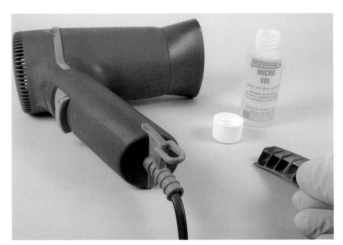

Drier used when applying decals. It can also be used to accelerate the drying time of paint.

4. EQUIPMENT

4.1 What basic equipment should I have?

As well as tools, all kinds of easily affordable home products can be utilised. Many are as useful as tools and make any job that much easier.

A spray bottle filled with water is useful both for cleaning and for 'wetting down' an area so that specks of dust are prevented from contaminating a part that is to be painted.

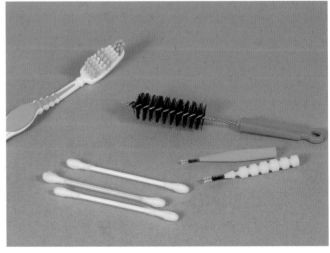

Cotton buds and different size brushes are excellent for cleaning tools and removing dust and paint residue.

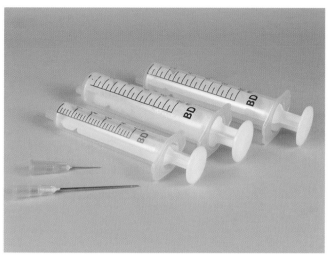

Hypodermic needles are useful for mixing the correct paint proportions, injecting resin, making aerials, etc.

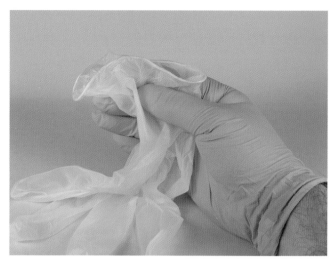

Vinyl or nitrile gloves are indispensable for avoiding paint stains or preventing the transference of contaminants to painted surfaces.

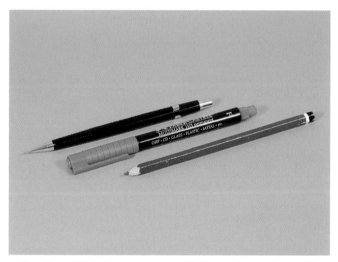

Pencils and felt tip pens are useful for making notes on kit instructions, marking defects on a model. Pencil lead is also very useful for adding special effects to an engine.

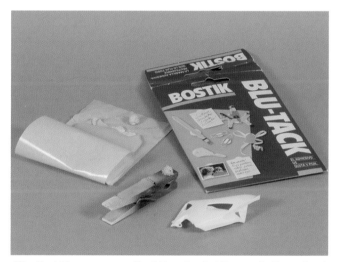

'Blu-Tack' is a very practical item for holding parts throughout the painting process, or as a mask, as it will not 'lift' the paint and leaves no residue when removed.

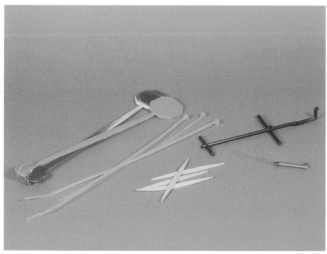

Lots of other items, like tooth picks or plastic rod are perfect for holding parts during painting, or paint removal, etc.

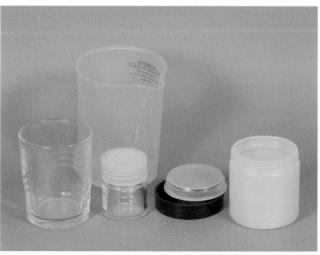

Glass or special plastic receptacles are useful for mixing chemicals or paints that could otherwise damage other plastic.

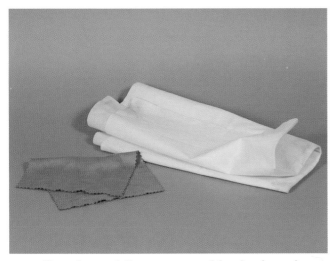

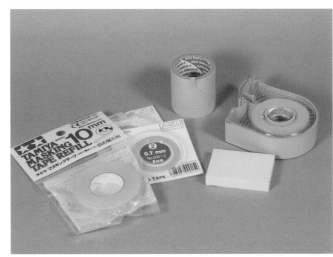

Glass cleaner cloths are very good for cleaning and polishing surfaces as they are made of anti-static fabrics, thus preventing dust and other particles from being attracted to plastic parts.

Adhesive low-tack masking tapes. Use only those tapes that are specifically designed for modelling as they will not 'lift' the paint when removed.

5. ABRASIVE PAPER

5.1 What are grade sizes?

Being able to choose the suitable paper for a particular operation is a key factor in obtaining a high quality finish.

The enormous range of abrasive papers is conveniently rated according to grade size. On the reverse of the sheet of abrasive paper is a printed code giving the grade number. The lower the grade number, the higher the abrasive power, i.e. 400 grade paper will be more abrasive than 1200.

5.2 What types of Wet'n'Dry paper are there?

Common and Polishing

Reverse of abrasive Wet 'n' Dry paper: note the grade number.

5.3 What abrasive papers should I have?

Common abrasive papers
- 400 grade, exclusively for removing flaws on resin and white metal surfaces
- 600 grade or 800 grade should just be used to remove flaws on plastic surfaces

- 1200grade for putties and priming
- 1500grade up to 2000grade for painted surfaces and finishing

Polishing abrasive paper
- These are available as a set or singly. As a set they come in the following grades, 3200, 3600, 4000, 6000, 8000 and 12000 (the operational process is fully explained in Point 17).

Abrasive papers for polishing lacquers and varnishes. They are sold together as a set to accomplish the whole process.

5.4   What is the correct abrasive papering process?

The first step is to know the correct Wet'n'Dry paper to use so as not to leave, at all costs, any scratches and imperfections that will still be visible when the item is later painted. The next step is to soak the Wet'n'Dry paper in water and begin the process, sanding with fingers in a vertical position, moving left to right, not up and down as we unconsciously apply unequal pressure with the middle finger. When sanding very small parts, the process is the same but only the forefinger is used.

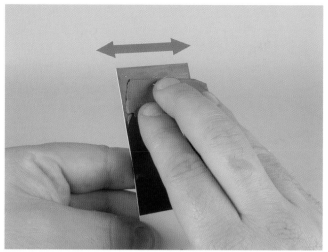

The correct sanding movement using a lateral finger movement.

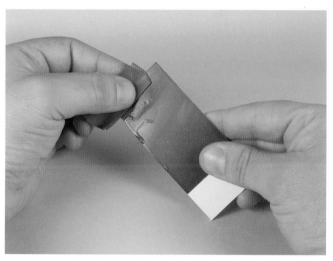

Incorrect sanding using the thumb.
This digit is uncontrollable and will result in oversanding.

Marks left when using the incorrect abrasive paper.
These will be difficult to cover up.

5.5   Some advice

• When using bodywork putty (Point 9, Section 9.3), avoid using Wet'n'Dry papers as this type of filler contains talcum that retains water. When applying paint later, this retained moisture will be released and the paint will crack. For this reason, always use 'dry' abrasive paper for flattening this type of surface.
• It is best to cut sandpapers into strips, marking each strip with its grade number on the reverse.
• To remove flaws on tyres, a 'Scotch Brite' pad is the best solution.
• Throughout the sanding process, always use one abrasive paper after another and never 'jump over' a grade. For example, if you are working with a 600 grade paper it should not be followed with a 1500 grade paper.

Strips of abrasive paper with grade number
on the reverse for future reference.

Using a Scotch Brite pad
to erase a tire flaw.

6. *INSPECTING AND STUDYING A KIT*

When purchasing a new kit, without doubt one of life's more thrilling moments, the first thing to do is to carefully check what is inside: parts, photo-etch sheets, decals, instructions, etc. After that, comes the process of evaluating its complexity and how much enjoyment will be gained from it.

After this first 'contact' comes the job of carefully checking that nothing is missing and that all parts are present along with the instruction sheet. Should any part be missing, do not hesitate to return the kit to the shop or manufacturer for the mistake to be rectified. Most specialist shops are more than happy to put any omission or fault right.

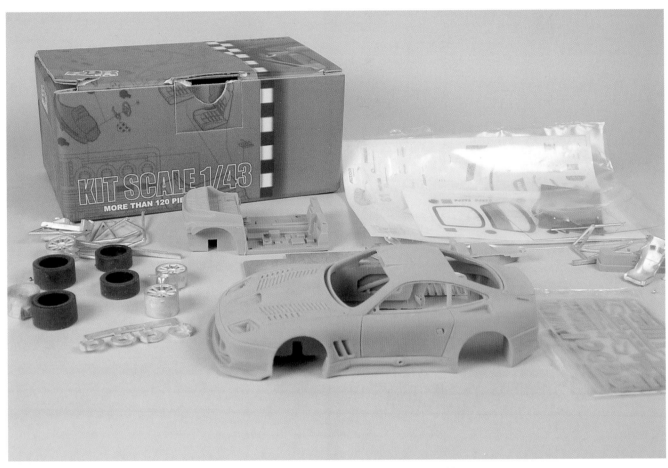

All the parts are removed from the box for checking.

6.1 What are the first steps to follow?

Once you are sure that all the parts are there, they should be stored - especially the small ones- in sealed containers to ensure that they are kept safe. A good method is to purchase a number of plastic containers with several compartments. They can be found in most DIY stores.

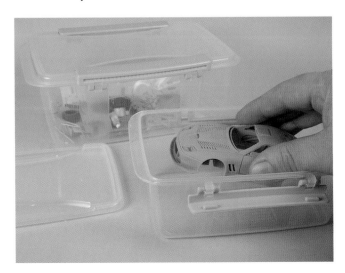

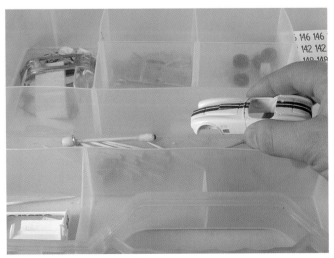

Some kits include alternative variants, including different drivers, colours, etc. At this juncture, it is important to obtain as much reference about all the variants before making the final decision as to what variant to model, Grand Prix, Rally, race, year, etc.

All the references should be mounted on a board and kept close at hand.

It is not always necessary to follow the manufacturer's assembly sequences as laid down in their instructions. In my case, I usually begin with the bodywork or fairing (in the case of a motorcycle) whenever possible. This decision should be made after a close study of the instructions and all related parts.

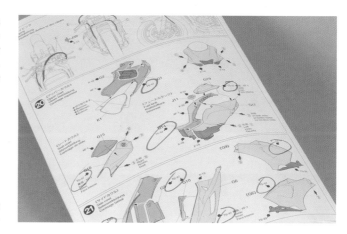

A selection of parts to be painted in the same colour.

Some kits include chromium plated parts. These can either be left as they are or repainted with 'Chrome effect' paint. It's your choice.

'Chromium plating' can removed with nitric acid, caustic soda, or other drain-cleaning products available from any supermarket. The product is first mixed with water in a container and the chromium-plated part then left to soak for a few minutes. Do not forget to wear protective gloves.

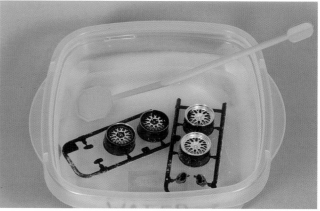

7. ELIMINATING FLAWS AND MAKING THE FIRST IMPROVEMENTS

Once the kit has been inspected, it should be checked against all the available references to make sure it is as accurate as possible. It must then be checked for any manufacturing faults, and this can be quite a job as it includes eliminating mould 'sink' marks, and carrying out any number of basic improvements, taking into account the three basic kit materials: plastic, resin and white metal.

7.1   Checking for imperfections

All parts should be inspected for mould lines, flaws, scratches etc.

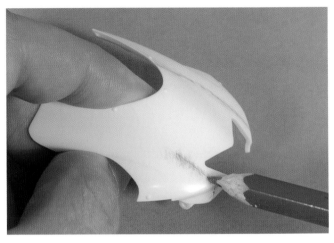

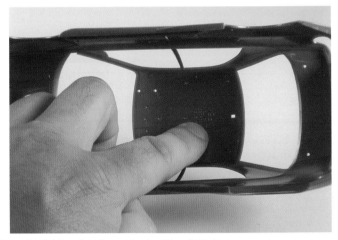

Once any flaws and imperfections are spotted, they should be clearly marked with a felt-tip pen or pencil before any further action is taken, such as applying filler or sanding.

Following sanding, any residue can be removed with a toothpick.

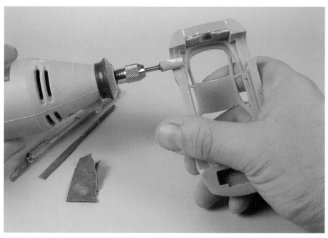

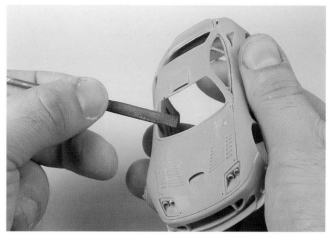

Depending of the extent of the imperfection, they can be eliminated with the use of files or a mini-drill fitted with a milling bit.

White metal parts can be burnished with a steel or rubbed with steel wool after sanding smooth.

7.2 How to improve the bodywork?

There are quite a few initial improvements that can be made to the bodywork that cannot be implemented later without risking damage to already completed areas.

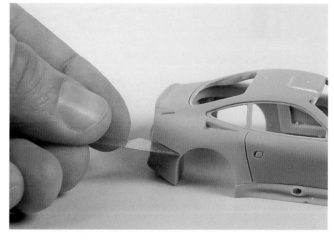

Sometimes, low quality, or cottage industry kits have panel lines that are badly marked or scarcely engraved. Using a sharp pointed instrument or photo-etched saws, they can be improved or even re-engraved if necessary.

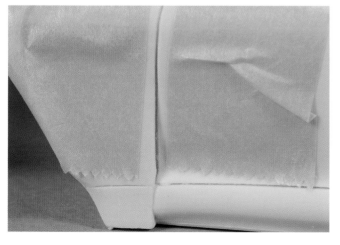

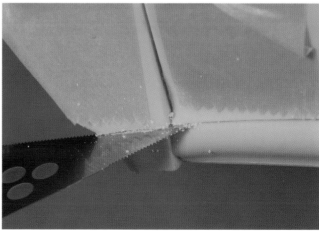

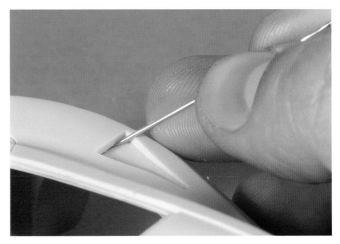

Where air ducts are not well defined or need to be deepened, these can also be improved. To do this, use a needle to mark a shallow guide and then, using drills or files open out the duct until the required width and depth has been achieved. Finally, the thickness of the duct may need to be thinned to bring it into scale. Use a sharp scalpel blade for this.

If the exhaust pipes are not well defined, they can be replaced with suitable lengths of metal tubing of the same diameter.

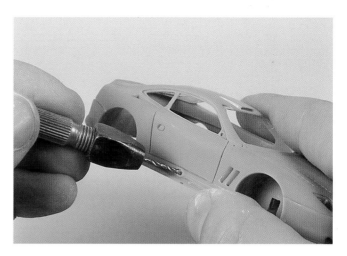

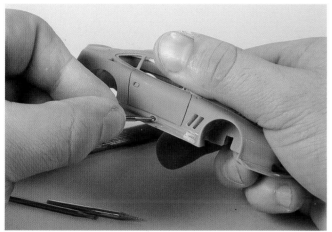

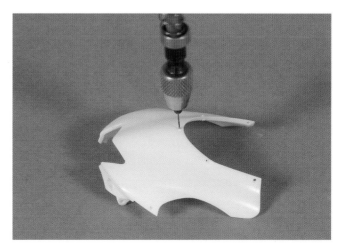

The thickness of the paint or lacquer may cover any engraved rivet lines. The solution here is to mark their position with tiny drill holes and apply replacements later.

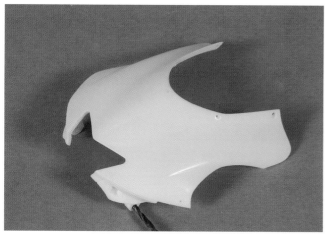

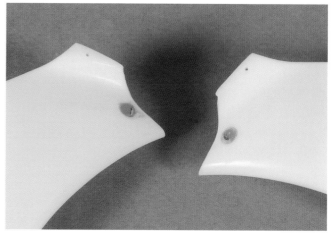

If an assembly bolt or nut is too visible, it can be integrated into the bodywork.
The hole will have to be enlarged to achieve a proper fit.

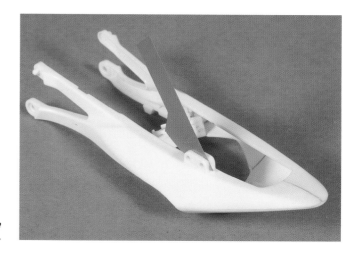

Some of the parts may be out-of-scale thick, but these can be
thinned with a sharp scalpel blade or photo-etched blades.

Depending on hardness of the material, over-thick parts can
also be thinned with files and milling bits.

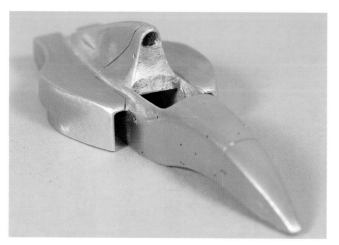

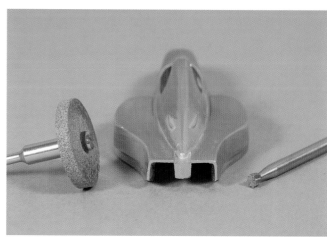

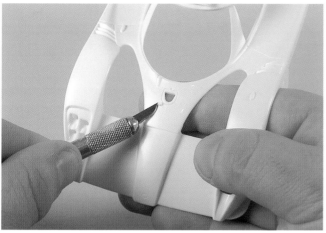

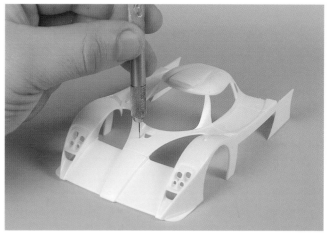

Aerials and other complementary small parts can be removed and their position marked for replacement at a later stage.

8. CEMENTS

At this point, there is no need to go into a definition of glue, we are all well aware what their purpose is. The problem here is rather to know what type should be used for each particular operation. At this point, we will explain what are the most usual modelling glues and offer some advice as to their use.

8.1 Cements for plastic kits

Most common type. These are easy to apply, are clean, although some care is required when gluing painted parts.

Easy application by means of a small brush included in the cap.

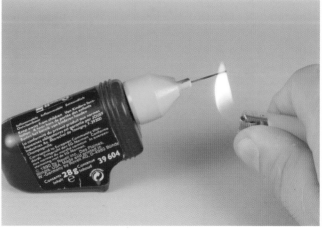

Some glue containers are equipped with a hollow dispenser tube. If the tube becomes blocked, heat it with a lighter and the dried glue inside will melt, thus restoring a free flow of glue. It can also be cleared with a fine wire.

8.2 Universal solvent

This solvent can be used as a polystyrene glue for the plastic used in most models (this will, incidentally, also save some money). Great care should be taken when applying it to painted parts.

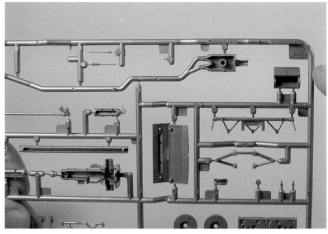

On most plastic kits, the sprue frames are marked with the type of plastic they are made from. Universal solvent can be used for all kits marked (PS).

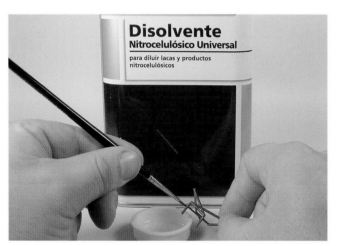

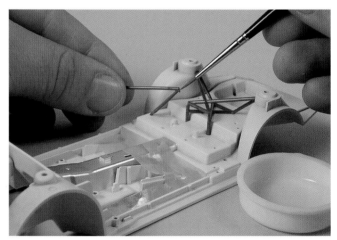

Solvent is sparingly applied with a brush.

8.3 Cyanoacrilate glue

Usually known nowadays as superglue, it is a instantly setting glue used for joining parts that need to resist weight or movement. It has to be used carefully, as there is no room for mistakes because of its extremely fast setting time. In addition, vapour is produced during the setting process and this has to be taken into account when gluing painted parts. This type of glue is not suitable for use with transparent plastics.

When using superglue, the less the better. Apply only very small quantities of glue as its adherence decreases, and may even completely disappear if too is applied.

Cyanoacrilate gel can also be used. This type of superglue has a slower setting time and a pasty texture. Use it in the same way as the traditional type, although it will allow for small corrections.

Cyanoacrilate and cyanoacrilate gel.

The mechanical resistance of the glue can be increased by adding a thickening agent, i.e. bicarbonate, to get a thicker mixture.

8.4 Wood glue

The most versatile glue, and one used more and more. It can be diluted with water, becomes transparent when dry, has very high adherence properties and leaves no residue. If, by chance, a part needs to be detached, any glue residue can easily be removed. In addition, it is very economical and easy to find, even at stationery shops under the heading of white glue for children.

It is very good for gluing already painted parts, transparent parts and even photo-etched components (brass parts).

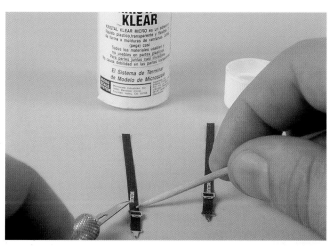

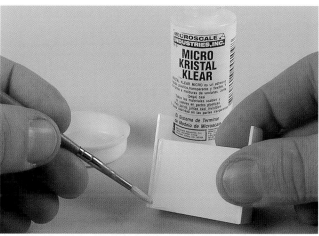

Different wood glue uses. When diluted with water it can be applied with a brush.

8.5 Two-component cement

The primary characteristic of this glue is its great mechanical resistance. This is the result of mixing two components in equal proportions. The strength of the glue is impaired if the mixing proportions are altered.

It is only used in specific cases to withstand high pressure.

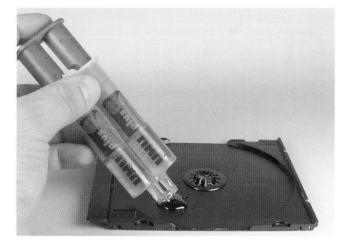

These glues are sold with double dispensers allowing an identical quantity of each component to be squeezed for exact mixing.

9. LEVELLING SURFACES

All kits on the market have imperfections that have to be rectified if a perfect model is to be realised. To achieve this, different types of filler will have to be used dependent on the material that the kit is made of and the size of the problem.

Different types of filler.

9.1 How different are fillers?

The primary difference is that some set at room temperature, while others set by a chemical reaction that is released when a catalyst is mixed with a base component.

9.2 What are the pros and cons of fillers that set at room temperature?

The main advantage is that they can be applied straight from the container. On the other hand, the disadvantages are that they do not set hard enough and also lose shape as the solvent evaporates. This type of filler should only be used for small imperfections.

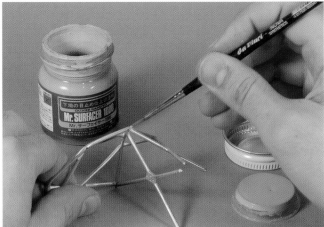

9.3 What are the pros and cons of chemical setting fillers?

The best pro is their hardness when set and their wonderful qualities of adherence on most surfaces; they are the more versatile and highly dependable. Depending on the manufacturer, they are generally the result of mixing two components.

They are mainly used for larger jobs.

This is mixed at a 98% filler–2% hardener until a homogeneous colour is achieved.

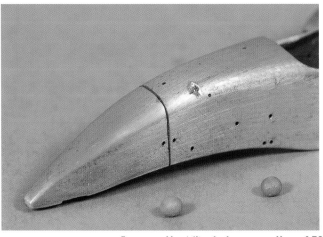

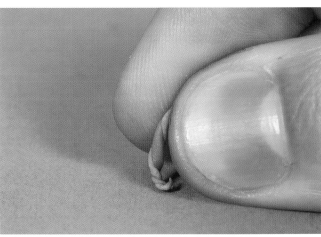

Epoxy putty. Mixed at a proportion of 50:50 until a homogeneous colour is obtained.

9.4   Can cement be used as filler?

Yes, but not all. The best ones are those that do not lose too much shape when set. The fastest and more stable setting glue is cyanoacrilate, better known as superglue. This can be used by itself directly or after adding bicarbonate. The chemical reaction means that it sets almost immediately.

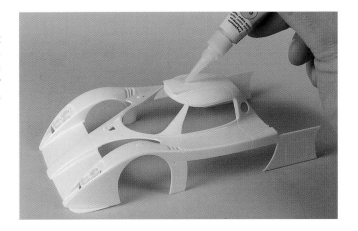

9.5   How to sand filler?

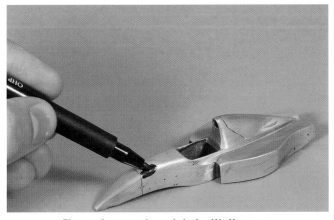

The surface can be painted with the same paint as the rest of the part thus making obvious the areas to be sanded.

During sanding keep checking for any surface imperfections.

To complete the sanding operation, finish with a very fine grade abrasive.

10. PRIMING

10.1 What is priming?

Priming is a coat of paint designed to protect the piece and increase paint adherence. Without first priming a part, the paint may not set properly and might eventual peel off. In addition, priming helps to level the surface and acts as an aid for checking flaws

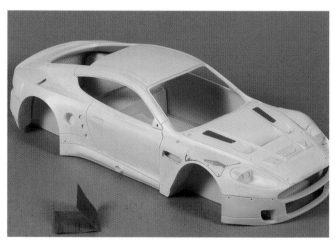

There are several types of primer. Some of them are specific for given materials, while others are multi-purpose because of their greater surface adherence and are perfect for both resin and metal kits.

10.2 How to prime?

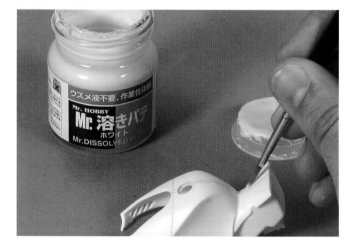

Some primers can be applied with a brush and are suitable for specific points requiring levelling or concealing defects. Once dry, they can be sanded with a fine grade abrasive paper.

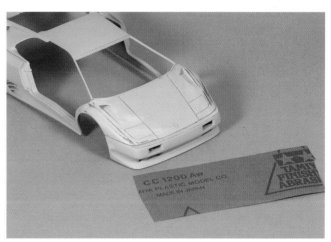

Some primers can be thinned with universal solvent, which allow them to be used with an airbrush.
The surfaces can be sanded smooth after the application of a number of coats. Always use a fine grade sandpaper.

Some spray primers can also be used. The colour of the primer used is dependent on the final colour of the piece. For example, colours such as red, blue and yellow are intensified and look better over a white primer.

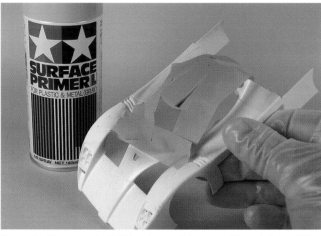

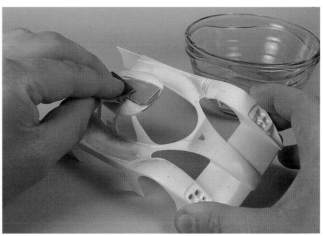

Imperfections can be hidden by masking specific points and then rubbing down using a fine grade abrasive sheet between each coat.

Paint does not adhere very well to metal. For that reason, a high adherence primer is required. Level all the surfaces using fine grade paper after each coat until a satisfactory result is achieved.

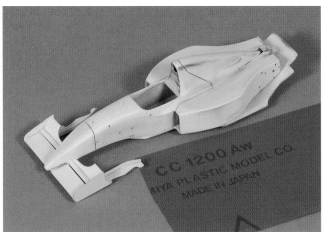

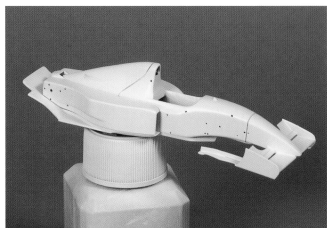

11. PAINTING STANDS

11.1 Why use a stand?

The primary reason for using a stand during painting is to avoid handling with bare hands, as skin retains grease and dirt and this will react with the paint, causing it to either peel off or bubble.

11.2 How parts can be held?

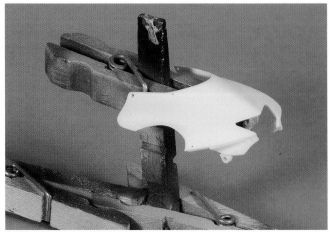

With metal, plastic or wooden tweezers.

By rolling pieces of adhesive tape, leaving the adhesive side up, small parts can be held satisfactorily during painting.

Sticking parts with Blu-Tack.

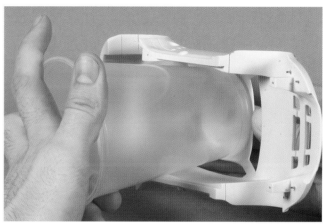

Sticking with Blu-Tack on containers or steadier stands.

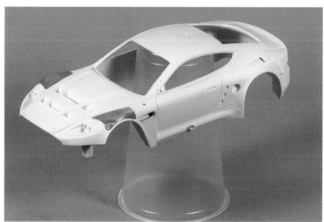

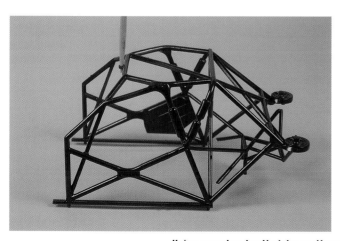

Using wooden toothpicks as they are conical and can be introduced through holes until a firm hold on the part is obtained.

With heat-stretched plastic sprue used in the same way as a toothpick, but in smaller holes.

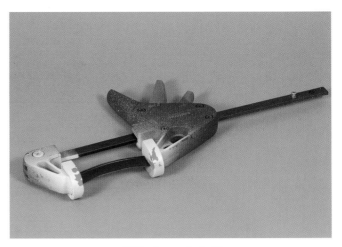

With clamps to hold the parts by the ends.

12. **COMPRESSORS AND AIRBRUSHES**

12.1 What is a compressor?

A compressor is a machine that supplies air at a pressure strong enough to allow the use of airbrushes.

12.2 Which one is the most suitable?

Put quite simply, one that meets your particular requirements. If just an airbrush is to be used, air consumption will be low and the required pressure does not need to exceed 2 bar (29 psi), thus a large compressor is not required…any one will do.

On the other hand, if it is going to be required for long sessions, a compressor equipped with an air reservoir tank will be required to avoid the machine working continuously to deliver a steady air supply.

If a spray gun, rather than an airbrush, is used, the air consumption will noticeably increase up to an average of 110-150 litres per minute, and a larger capacity compressor will thus be required.

The compressor chosen should be equipped with a plate detailing its technical data.

Contrary to popular belief, air pressure is not a key factor, as a modeller will always work at a lower pressure than that supplied by most compressors. The most important feature is the potential airflow.

A typical compressor plate. It can be seen that the flow is 160 ltr/min, which is above that required for the spray gun used here (110 ltr/min). The plate also shows an 8 bar maximum pressure (116 psi), far above what is normally required.

Some compressors are fitted with manometers. In the photograph, the left manometer registers internal pressure, while the right one indicates exit pressure, which is controlled by the operator and shown by the pressure gauge above.

12.3 What types of compressors are available?

• Membrane compressors

These are smaller and more economical, although the pressure values and, above all, airflow, fluctuate a bit. They are not really recommended for extended use. Also, they allow no control over the exit pressure.

• Alternating compressors

The best choice. They are fitted with a air reservoir tank, pressure gauge, safety valves, and manometers, and offer all possibilities for airflow and pressure. However, they are, of course, bigger and noisier than the previous ones. In addition, they are that much more expensive.

Included among this type are also the oil-less compressors, requiring no lubrication oil. These are surely the best type because if oil should find its way into the paint feed, the paint will be contaminated and we will have a problem as covered in Section 17.

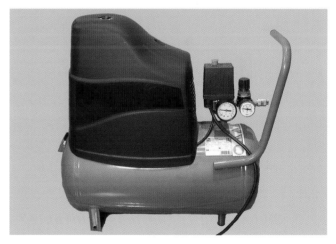

12.4 What is an airbrush?

It is a small paint gun able to draw a thin line.

12.5 Which is the most recommended?

Quite obviously, a good quality one, even for beginners. This is a piece of equipment that should last a lifetime when properly cared for. A good quality airbrush will save much time and problems, and will make an easier learning curve. Finally, the more you work with it, the more you will enjoy its versatility.

There are many manufacturers supplying airbrushes and, for that reason, we will not indicate which ones are good or bad as this is rather subjective. Nevertheless, we will underline the more important criteria to assist you in making the correct choice for you. The first factor is price, it is important not to try to save too much when purchasing this piece of equipment. There are quite good, affordable airbrushes at reasonable prices. Another significant factor is to ensure that the supplier you choose is able to supply you with a good range of spare parts, such as nozzles, needles and, hopefully, a complete catalogue of accessories and they are readily available. In addition, you should ensure that all the joints, washers, O-rings, etc, are made of Teflon that allow the use of any type of paint and subsequent nitro-cellulose cleaning solvent. If you choose an airbrush fitted with rubber joints, it will limit the paints and cleaning products you can use.

Last, but not least, your airbrush must be a double action model, which allows you to control the air and paint flows independently.

For example, we use a Badger 100, a Badger 150 and a Paasche VL airbrushes.

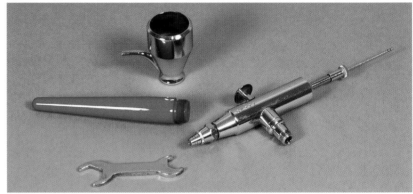

Several types or airbrush with some accessories. The majority of quality airbrushes have three nozzles with their respective needles, normally 0.3, 0.5 and 0.7mm.

Often the components that succumb most to the effects of wear are the needle and nozzles. These can be easily replaced, thus restoring the airbrush to perfect working order.

Two-trigger positions of a double-action airbrush, pushing down for air flow and to the rear for paint.

12.6 How should the paint be diluted?

Paint to be sprayed through an airbrush has to be diluted. This is achieved by adding a specific solvent to make it more fluid and thinner. There is no fixed rule to determine how much solvent must be used except that laid down by the airbrush manufacturer. On the other hand, air pressure and spraying range are key factors in the final result. That is to say, only through practice can you acquire the desired skill. To attain this level of skill demands that you spend some time in trial and error exercises to become completely familiar with your airbrush.

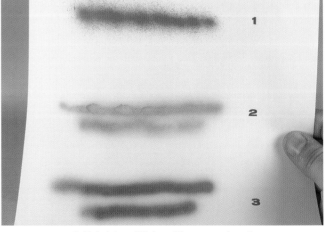

1. Paint too thick, add more solvent.
2. Paint too thin, add more paint.
3. Just right!

12.7 How should the airbrush be cleaned?

The primary reason for an airbrush to work badly (except if it is dropped or been knocked) is dirt. To remedy this, it is necessary to take it completely apart and give it a thorough cleaning before use. Well, why not! Once we have finished painting with a particular colour and before starting with another, the paint cup must be emptied and cleaned by pouring in some alcohol or solvent and spraying this into a container filled with water until the paint cup is completely empty. Finally, to ensure that there is no paint residue at all, pour a little more alcohol into the paint and, this time, spray onto a clean sheet of paper.

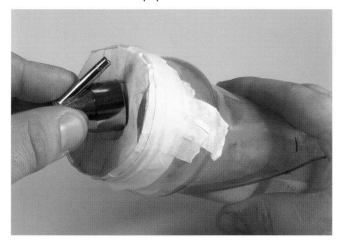 

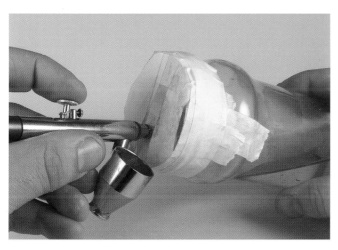 

When all airbrush work has been completed, the time has arrived for a thorough cleaning. It should be completely taken apart and thoroughly cleaned.

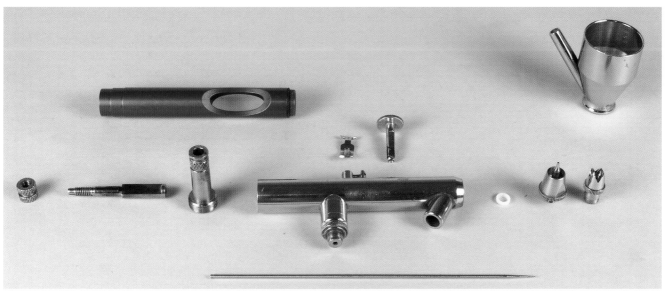

The airbrush fully disassembled.

The airbrush paint gate is cleaned using
a cotton bud soaked in alcohol.

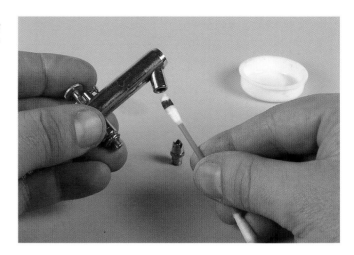

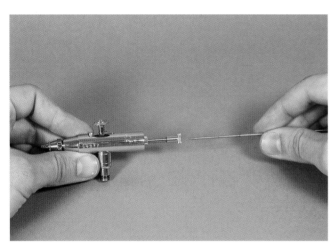

The needle is removed and cleaned on a piece of paper, also soaked in alcohol.

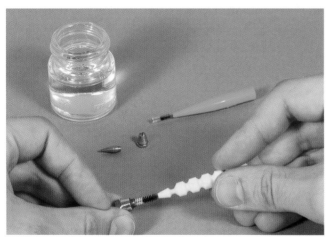

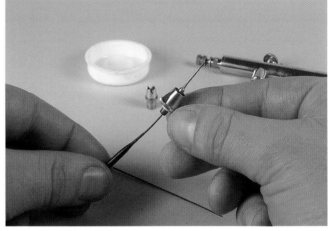

The nozzle is cleaned with small tooth brushes. Fine heat-stretched plastic sprue
is useful for cleaning the interior of the nozzle.

Frequently, paint residue will remain in the
paint cup pipe. Cleaning can be done using
solvent and a thick piece of string.

12.8 What are the most common problems with an airbrush?

More often than not, problems arise through lack of skill or the airbrush has not been cleaned properly. Here are a few of the more usual problems from a technical point of view.

Problem	Cause	Solution
Trigger is jammed	Dried paint on the needle	Cleaning
Needle is jammed	Damaged needle	New needle

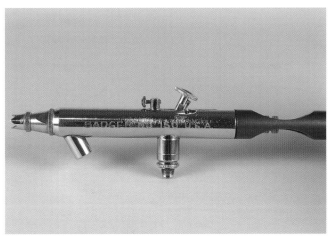

Note how the trigger is jammed: it doesn't return to its initial position after being pressed.

Problem	Cause	Solution
No paint	Paint too thick Not enough air pressure	Add solvent Raise the air pressure Check compressor hose or inlet air valve.
Bubbles in paint cup when pulling the trigger	Dirty nozzle	Clean nozzle

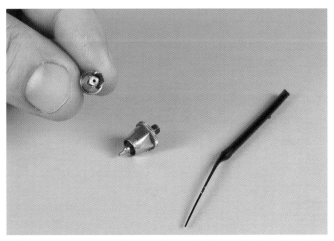

Dirty nozzle orifices. The solution is to clean the interior of the orifices with soft, nap-free material.
Air doesn't blow through the nozzle when it is assembled but, instead, blows out from paint cup.

Problem	Cause	Solution
When pulling the trigger for air paint also blows	Needle is fitted wrong or is worn out	Re-fit or re-place needle

To fit the needle, first loosen the adjusting nut and gently draw needle to the top. It is advisable to place the rear protector to prevent any damage to the needle if it should be dropped.

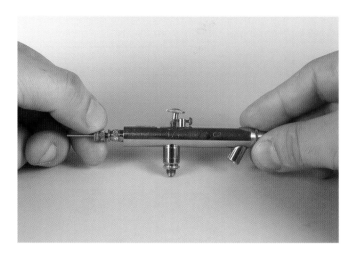

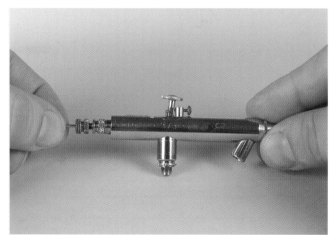

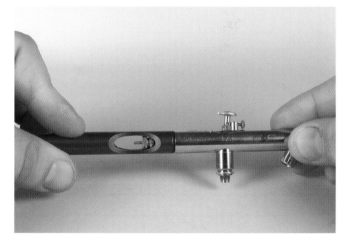

Problem	Cause	Solution
Leakage and bubbling around nozzle	Loose nozzle or damaged watertight joint	Tighten nozzle or replace joint

Teflon watertight joint.

13. BODYWORK PAINTS

13.1 Introduction

In this section, we will look at the different paints available on the market, and review the advantages and disadvantages of each of them. In addition, we will attempt to give some advice for selecting the most suitable one for each particular case.

It is important to point out, that all paints reviewed can be safely lacquered or varnished.

13.2 What types of paint are available?

• Specific modelling paints.
• Professional car paints.

13.3 What are specific modelling paints?

These are all those paints that can easily be found in any specialist model shops. The primary disadvantage with these paints is that the range of colours can still be pretty limited, especially so in the case of cars.

They can be divided into the following categories:

• Spray cans.
• Enamels.
• Acrylics.

• What is a spray can?

Spray cans are very handy and easily used as they require no cleaning and are a good substitute for airbrushes. Coverage is usually quite good with just a couple of coats.

They should be sprayed at a distance of around 20cm, avoiding saturation. It is much better to apply additional coats as required, keeping each coat as thin as possible.

The disadvantages of these, is that the paint is toxic and too much of it is wasted during the painting process. In consequence, they should always be used in well-ventilated areas and a protective mask should always be worn.

The trick is not to over apply the paint, but gently spray at a convenient distance and never get too close to the model. If a higher pressure is required, heat the spray can in a container filled with hot water or, in the winter, simply place it on a radiator for a while.

To avoid paint wastage, spray the paint into a suitable container or directly into the airbrush reservoir and then paint in the usual way. If this is done, the paint does not need to be diluted.

• What is enamel?

This type of paint is airbrushed and diluted with a specific thinner. The paint should first be well stirred inside its container before being diluted. The colour range is somewhat limited for bodywork.

In addition, they are toxic, smell foul, and are slow drying. The airbrush can be cleaned with universal solvent.

• What is an acrylic paint?

The advantage with these paints is that they can be diluted with water, although there are also specific solvents available. They have little odour; can be applied with an airbrush or, in some cases, with a brush, although always remember that the best finish is obtained with an airbrush. The colour range is also limited.

There are also available other different textured paints such as the ones used by figure painters, and these can also be used with brush or airbrush.

In this case, an acrylic fluorescent paint has been used to paint the mirrors on a Alfa Romeo 155 DTM. Fluorescent colours require a white undercoat. For this job, the white primer would be later airbrushed in a fluorescent green, although this type of paint can also be hand brushed. The final operation is to give it a coat of gloss varnish.

13.4 What are professional car paints?

One of the pleasures of painting cars or motorcycles is, without doubt, matching them with the correct, original colour. At times, finding the correct colour shade can be very difficult, but it is worth the effort especially when comparing the finished model with the full scale original.

The primary advantage of these paints is that they are easily (usually!) obtained in the correct colour and the range is practically unlimited.

In actuality, all cars have a universal code identifying its colour. This code guarantees that neither the colour tone nor saturation will change if it needs to be repainted. As an example, there are many variations for Ferrari red, but if a check is made on a Ferrari 360 Modena a FER 300 universal code will be found and this is the correct colour match.

Sometimes, the actual colour is written in the kit instructions, which makes it all so much easier. In this case, the code is blue Renault 409 from the year 1988 and was used to paint the Ferrari 550 Maranello shown in these pages.

The greatest difficulty with this type of paint is how to obtain them, as they are not available in model shops (although there are some manufacturers that offer specific codes in small jars). So, to acquire these paints, it is necessary to go to a bodyshop, or a specialist car paint shop. However, the one drawback with these paints is that, usually, they are not available in quantities of less than 100 grams weight (50 grams are enough to paint four 1/24 models). Then again, the price, when compared with modelling paints, is far cheaper, resulting in significant savings.

Vehicle paints are:

• Mono-coat.

• Two-pack.

• Wave.

• What is a mono-coat paint?

These are no longer used in the auto industry, but can, at times, still be found. This paint is composed of a colour, a drying catalyser and thinner. All these components make a deep, glossy, highly resistant coat. They are only used for solid, non-metallic colours.

Painting with a mono-coat paint. Notice the gloss and depth. In this particular case, this is a competition model with decals. A lacquer coat -mono-coat paint is impervious to and wont be damaged by lacquer- was applied later.

• What is a two-pack paint?

As opposed to mono-coat paint, with two-pack paint only colour is applied and lacquer is then applied over it to get the desired gloss and consistency. Thus, the process is accomplished in two phases. Drying is instantaneous. They have to be diluted at 50% with an specific solvent and can be airbrushed. The finish is completely flat.
Solid, metallic and even pearl finishes are possible.
For metallic colours, our advice is to apply the final coat at low pressure and remain at a greater distance so that metal specks, being heavier than colour pigments, fall on the surface and remain in the same position to render a uniform tone.

The flat finish of this type of paints is very noticeable. They are applied in two or three coats.

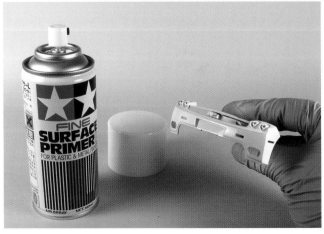

As a general rule, a good cover of white primer should be applied to enhance some particular colours. In this case, additional coats were needed to give real depth to the yellow.

• What is a wave?

Nowadays, these are the most common paints used in body shops. Their main advantage is that they are non-toxic and have a low pollution rate because of their low VOC (volatile organic compounds). Although they are designed for use with specific solvents, tap water can also be used. There is little doubt that these paints have replaced both mono-coat and two-pack. Modeller's shouldn't have any problem handling these paints as they behave very similarly to modelling acrylics. There is no problem in coating with lacquers or varnish.

The paint is diluted with water using a hypodermic needle in the correct proportion as laid down by the manufacturer.

When applying this paint, it soon becomes apparent that it has a very low odour.
The finish is satin and they are not fast drying.

The main disadvantage with this paint is that the actual colour will not be appreciated until the paint has completely dried. Some shades, like blues or dark greens, will look wrong at the beginning. However, have patience and wait until the paint is completely dry before checking the final result. To accelerate the drying process, a hair dryer can be used.

13.5 What safety measures should be taken?

Most of these paints are toxic so, consequently, care must be taken when using them and a suitable facemask is essential. It should also be remembered that paints give off vapours and not just paint droplets, so the mask must be furnished with a suitable filter.

The masks can either be the disposable type or have changeable filters. Whatever the case, they all work in the same way; basically, by mean of an active carbon agent to absorb the poisonous gases. The masks should be stored in a bag or the filter will deteriorate, thus shortening its service life. There is further information about disposable filters in Section 16 dedicated to lacquers.

Disposable mask: always keep the mask in its bag to ensure a long service life.

• When should a mask be changed?

When, after donning the mask, paint, lacquer, solvent etc, can be smelt through it.

14. APPLYING DECALS

14.1 Introduction

This can be one of the most discouraging items for the modeller, due to the fact that broken or badly applied decals on a racing vehicle (especially those carrying a large number of decals) can completely ruin a work. This will then necessitate, at worst, having to re-start the model or, at best, purchasing a new decal sheet with identical or similar motifs.

Decaling a racing vehicle is an operation than allows just a small margin of error. In this chapter, we shall explain some techniques and give some advice to realise the best results. It is obvious, however, that, at least, a modicum of experience is required and so it is highly recommended that beginners choose models that are not too complex and to test all new techniques on spare models in advance.

Another piece of advice is to always begin with the bodywork, it makes no sense to complete inner detail, i.e. engine, etc., without first making sure that the most difficult part, the bodywork, is finished to a satisfactory level in advance.

Before applying any decals it is very important to gloss varnish the whole bodywork, either with acrylic or enamel, sprayed or airbrushed. If this is not done, micro air bubbles can be trapped beneath the decal and these will remain visible.

Inside the Lion logo, the negative effect caused by not first applying a coat of varnish in advance can be clearly seen. This 'silvering' effect is due to the light reflecting on the trapped air bubbles.

14.2 What materials do I need for applying decals?

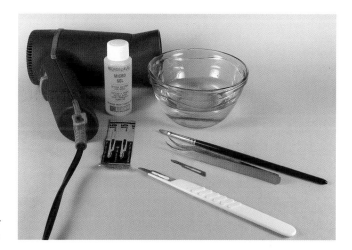

The basic requirements for the decaling operation.

14.3 How to apply simple decals?

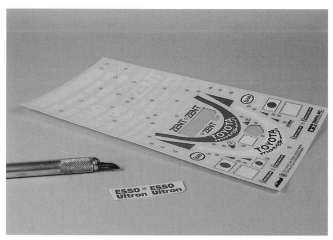

Begin by first trimming the carrier film from around the selected decal.

The decal is then placed into a container, a saucer is perfect, of clean water. After a few seconds, the decal will detach from the backing sheet. Using tweezers, position both the sheet and decal onto the model and slide the decal off with a brush.

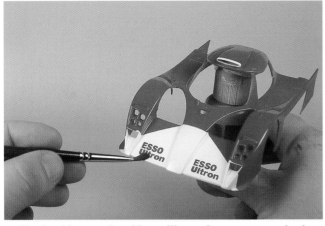

The decal is now placed in position and any excess water is removed by brushing across the decal's surface with the brush.

A hair drier is useful for speeding up the drying time and fixing the decal to surface. It is especially useful on uneven surfaces.

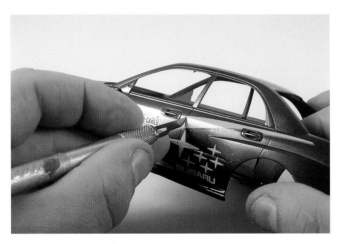

Using a new scalpel blade, it is important to trim decals around ducts or other openings.

A product for softening decals, Micro Sol is one such product, is applied in small measures and this will 'drag' the decal down onto any relief shape, so making it appear as an integral part of the model.

14.4 How to apply complex decals?

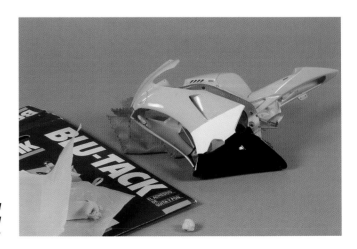

Often, some decals cover parts of the bodywork or fairing and extend along or around a large area and these are exceptionally difficult to apply because of their length.

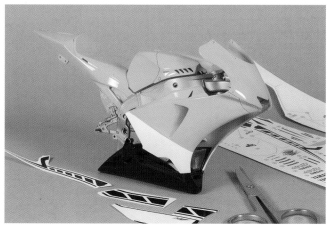

As in the previous case, the decal is trimmed from the sheet.

The decal is applied in the same way, although in this case, with some strategic cuts to make it conform to the shape of the part.

Using a brush, decal softener and a hair drier, proceed to the final fitting.

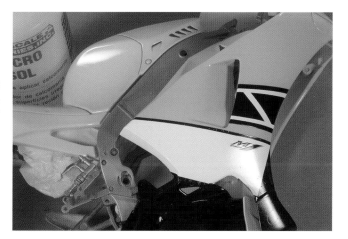

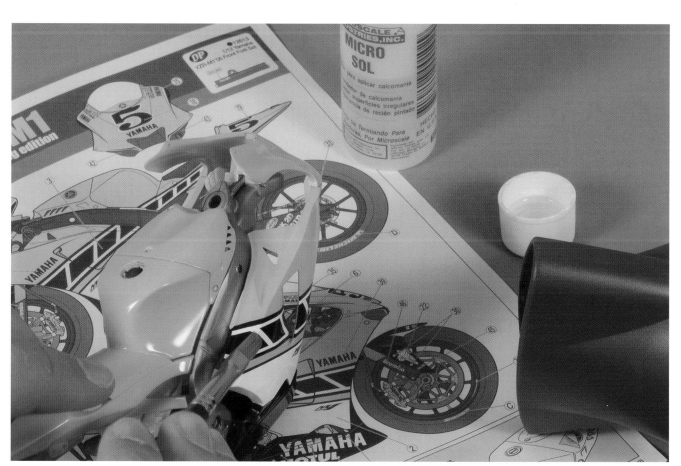

Carefully 'comb' the decal with a flat brush lightly soaked in water. If too much softener is added, the decal will shrink (this product should be applied exclusively to given points). To counterbalance this effect, more water can be added. It is recommended to use the instruction sheet as a guide when positioning the decals.

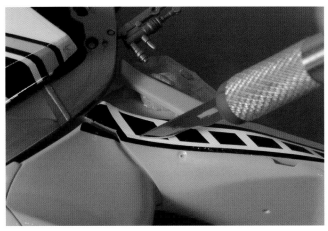

Decal is cut at the joint of two parts.

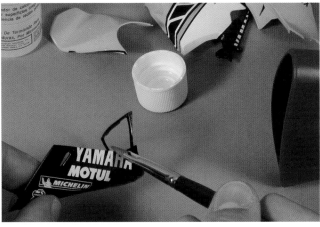

*Later, a decal softener is applied
to the edge of the part.*

The final result.

*This is an example of a complex kit, the whole bodywork is covered with decals,
with many of them having to be adjusted to each other.*

14.5 How to make patterns for decals?

The outline is drawn or traced onto a piece of paper.

The paper pattern is used to outline it onto the decal sheet of the correct texture; carbon fibre in this instance.

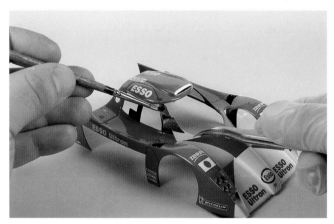

The decal is then applied in the same way as explained earlier.

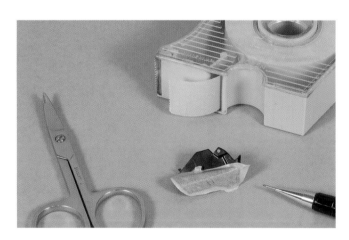

A pattern can also be made from masking tape.

The desired thread direction can be marked out with a pencil.

14.6 How should decals be stored?

Quite often, modellers hold a stock of models ready for the time when they can be assembled. In these circumstances, decals can be seriously damaged due to room temperature and moisture.

To keep decals moisture free, store in a box along with small bags of silica gel (moisture retainers) such as those found in boxes containing electronic equipment.

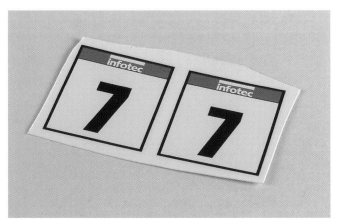

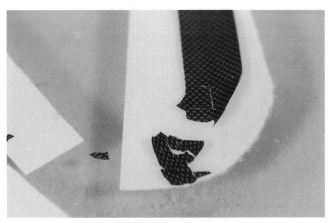

A typical example of decal damage: colour changes and cracking.

14.7 How to make decals?

Because not all alternative decorations wanted for a particular model are available (for example, a particular licence plate), these can be reproduced quite easily. There is available on the market a wide selection of software dealing with images and allowing for creation and design. The final result depends entirely on the experience and skill of the computer operator using these programs.

Personal photographs, scanning a particular logo or downloading an image from the internet will make the work easier.

The final design size should be determined, keeping to the correct scale.

Any printer can be used, although a laser printer is best as these fix the pigments using heating and the colour coat is thinner than with ink jet printers.

Once printed on paper, check that the dimensions are correct.

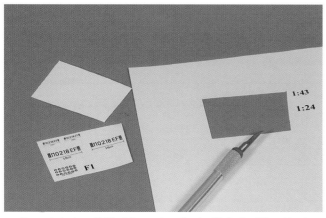

The printed motif is trimmed and substituted with a blank decal sheet available in most good model shops. Depending on requirements, transparent, white or a coloured sheet is used.

Using a piece of masking tape, the blank sheet is fixed. Be careful not to introduce any plastic adhesive inside a laser jet printer, as it will melt and cause damage.

The pattern is then printed onto the blank piece of decal sheet.

Once the decals are printed, a protective coat (once again, available in good model shops) is applied to protect and fix the printed design and thus prevent any damage when the time comes to soak it in water before applying it onto the model.

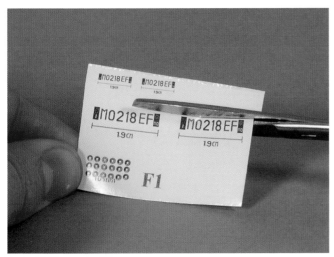

The decal is trimmed as required.

The final result.

15. *VARNISHING MODELS*

The most noticeable feature of any car bodywork is its high shine. In the next section, we will explain how to achieve this high shine through a simple, affordable process using varnish easily available from within the modelling industry.

15.1 How to varnish models?

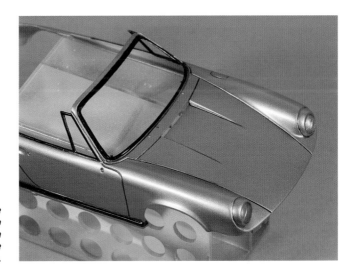

The first operation is to ensure that the bodywork is completely ready. That is to say, it has to be painted and detailed in advance, as the varnish could cover some detail on the bodywork.

Cover the part with an even coat of varnish from a distance of 20cm.
Do not attempt to do this with one thick coat, several thin coats are preferable.

Once this coat has dried, give it a second coat from the same distance. The purpose of these first coats is to avoid any chemical reaction that might be appear as a result of the spray solvents.

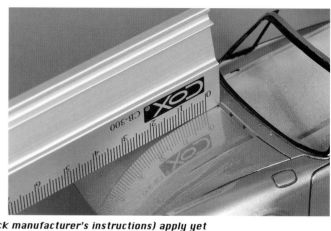

Once these coats have been applied (check manufacturer's instructions) apply yet another even varnish coat, this time at a distance of 12cm. A high gloss will now become apparent due to the increased quantity of varnish sprayed.

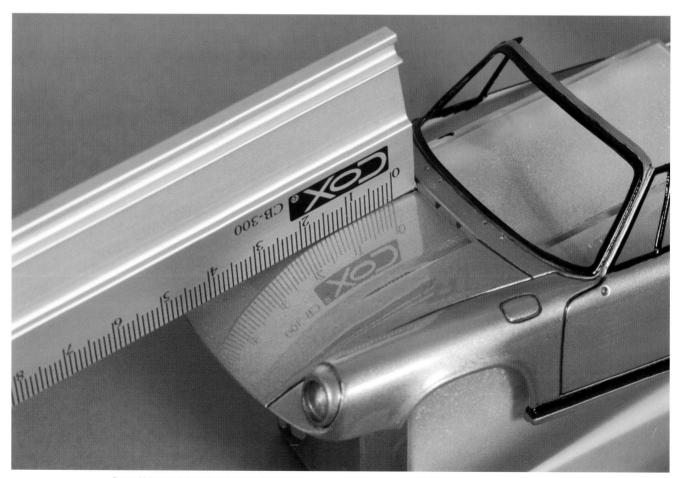

Once this coat has dried, give it yet another coat from same distance to increase the gloss.
Because this type of varnish has a low solid content, more coats have to be applied. As evaporation causes drying, which, incidentally, also affects the thickness of the different varnish coats, the end result is not as good as the method explained in Section 16.

16. LACQUER

Lacquer is a type of varnish that imparts a final gloss, while protecting the surfaces from external agents such as light, temperature or even ageing. The products used for this technique are identical to those used on full size vehicles..

16.1 Are these products really necessary?

No, but experience tells us that the finish obtained when using them is the best quality. Notwithstanding, there are many products available on the market giving a highly satisfactory result.

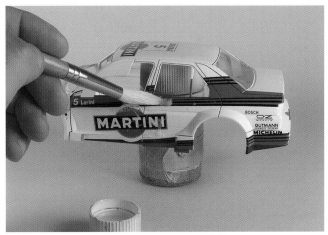

Before lacquer can be applied, all parts must be degreased. For this, a motor industry product can be used. However, failing that, soapy water and a brush and then rinsing with fresh water is almost as good.

16.2 What product should we use?

A combination of three products in pre-determined proportions: lacquer, catalyser and solvent.

• Lacquer

There are plenty of lacquer manufacturers operating in the motor industry. It is difficult to name the best, but be sure to use MS (medium solid contents) and not HS (high solid contents) as the coverage of the latter is liable to erase some details.

Different car lacquer manufacturers. Usually they are marketed in one kg containers and are on the pricy side, although we require just small quantities for painting models.

• Catalyser

Lacquer sets by chemical drying which means that another component is needed for it to reach a solid state. This product is called the catalyser, without it the lacquer will never set. There are also several types of catalyser, but the best is doubtless the slow drying one; the slower the drying time, the higher the gloss finish.

Catalyser is also sold in 1litre containers. It should be noted that these products age, so should be stored in a place with a constant temperature.

• Solvent or thinner

Solvent or thinner is used to make the mixture more fluid and easier to work with. The catalyser and solvent should never be confused as the latter de-ranges mixing.

16.3 How should the product be used?

As with any other similar case, the manufacturer's instructions (technical card in this case) should be closely followed.

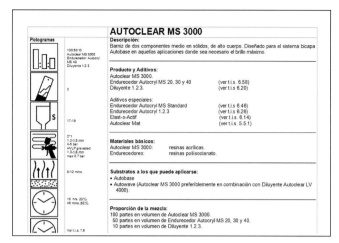

Limpieza del equipo:
Disolvente Sikkens, Diluyente 1.2.3 o Diluyente nitrocelulósico.

Tiempos de secado:	A 20°C:		
	MS 20	MS 30	MS 40
Seco al polvo:	35 min.	40 min.	45 min.
Seco al tacto:	3 hrs	3 hrs	4 hrs
Seco manejo:	7 hrs	8 hrs	10 hrs
Seco duro:	11 hrs	12 hrs	13 hrs
	A 60°C:		
	MS 20	MS 30	MS 40
Seco al polvo:	5 min.	5 min.	5 min.
Seco al tacto:	15 min.	20 min.	20 min.
Seco manejo:	20 min.	25 min.	30 min.
Seco duro:	30 min.	35 min.	45 min.

*Using the technical card, the correct mixing proportions can be checked for the three products,
also other technical data for related items, number of coats, drying times, cleaning products, etc.*

16.4 How should they be mixed?

According to the technical card, a 100/50/30 per cent proportion should be followed for lacquer, catalyser and thinner respectively. (Capacity measures).

*Mixing is easy when following
the manufacturer's instructions.*

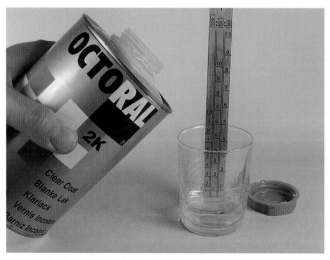

*The first step is to determine the mixing capacity. It will
usually be an approximate measure gained through experience,
but be generous and mix a little more than you feel is
necessary. In general, a small glass would be adequate for a
1/24 car with lacquer up to Level 2 in the left measure (100),
which is approximately 2 cm..*

*Next, add the catalyser. According to the proportion scale,
fill to Number 2 on central scale (50), and then
proceed in the same way with the solvent,
but on right scale, this time 30.*

All products must be well mixed and left to set for a few minutes before they are ready for use.

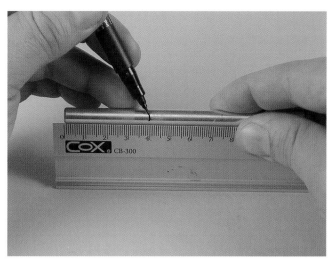

If you do not have a proportion scale to hand, a simple alternative can be made using the handle of a craft knife or any other metal material.

If the choice is 4 cm, 50% would be 2 cm more; that is, up to No.6 mark.

16.5 What protective equipment is required?

Protection is essential when using these toxic products. For that reason, there should also be good ventilation and a gasmask must be used.

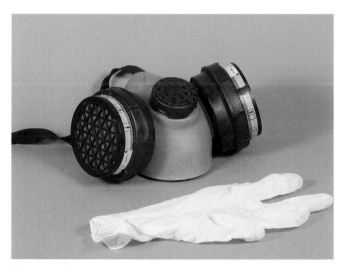

When buying a mask, care should be taken to check to see that it meets due regulations (EN-141 and 149 in Europe). This normally indicates which model is required and what type of gases it filters. Bodywork paints and lacquers both require masks fitted with brown filters.

16.6 How to apply the product?

The first thing to take note of is that a modicum of patience is required, as this is a rather complex process. Usually, the best results will not be obtained at the first attempt. This is normal as it does require a little practice. The best way is to practice on some other surfaces or spare parts until you feel you are ready to use this product on your model. However, once you have mastered its use, the result is very rewarding.

Lacquer can be used in a spray gun or airbrush. The following section explains when to use one or the other.

When painting large surfaces, like bodywork, a spray gun is much better and easier as it sprays paint in a larger pattern than an airbrush (which sprays in a conical, smaller pattern), and is also adjustable. To do the same job with an airbrush, more and faster coats would be required.

Spray guns need to be preset, as their use is somewhat of a personal choice. Here are a few settings as an easy starting reference.

The first step is to adjust the compressor's air pressure according to the instructions laid down by the lacquer manufacturer: 2.5 to 3 bars should be adequate. Next, adjust the spray pattern, as seen in the accompanying photograph. It is advisable to work with a spray pattern slightly larger than the part to be painted.

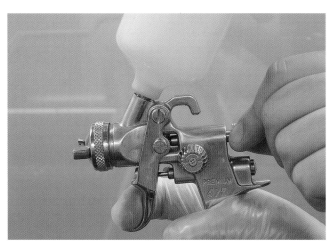
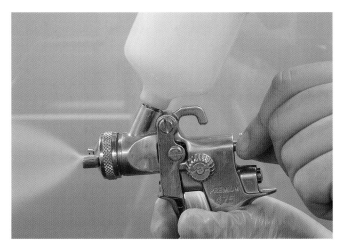

To adjust the quantity of lacquer to be sprayed, turn the screw shown in the photograph.
In fact, it is the nozzle's aperture that is being adjusted to allow more or less lacquer to pass through.

With the gun positioned parallel to the piece at a distance of approximately 20 cm, start by passing the gun back and forth at a rate that is comfortable for you and beginning and ending off the piece. This will give one coat. After approximately 5 minutes, apply a second coat. This technique is called 'humid on humid' as it is used in the motor trade. Immediately after all coats have been applied, the result might appear a little too thick. However, wait at least 24 hours to see the actual final result as the product shrinks significantly throughout its drying cycle.

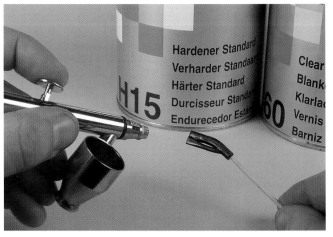

Small parts and even 1/43scale vehicles can be painted with the ever-versatile airbrush using the same application techniques.

16.7 How assemble and dismantle a spray gun?

To be able to carry proper maintenance, it is important to know in detail how to dismantle and clean the equipment.

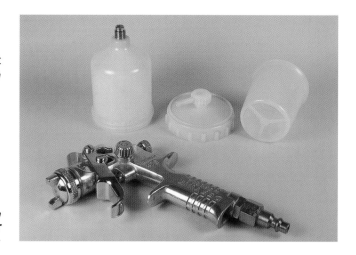

The paint cup consists of a filter and a cap with the air intake.

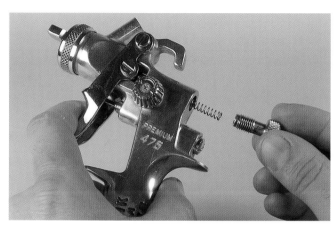

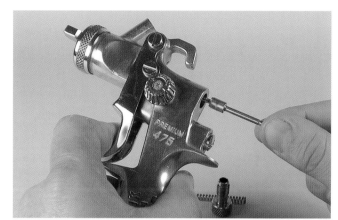

Needle extraction

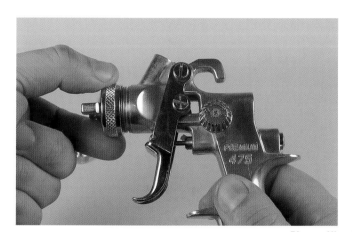

Dismantling the nozzle

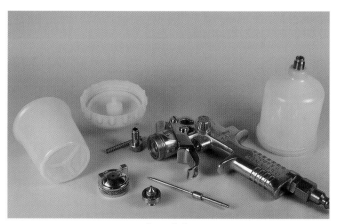

*Complete
break down*

*Using nitrocellulose and a brush, clean each part
and then blow them through with air pressure.*

Assembly is the reverse procedure to dismantling. Assemble the nozzle by first placing it on a horizontal surface.

Compare the difference between the spray and lacquer technique.

17. LACQUERING FLAWS

17.1 Introduction

Once the final parts and bodywork have been lacquered, some flaws or other defects may become obvious that ruin the whole model. In the speciality of vehicle modelling, unlike others, a high gloss, perfectly smooth surface is paramount. This implies a lot of care during work, as the viewer's attention will immediately be drawn directly to any flaw.

Despite the fact that there are around 22 typical flaws on the paintwork of any full-size vehicle, just 4 of them are common in modelling. It is these we will deal with in this section.

First, let us identify the flaws, their causes and subsequent solution. All the flaws treated in this section, although different, have, more or less, the same solution.

17.2 What are the typical flaws when lacquering or varnishing a model?

- Dust specks and dirt.
- Runs.
- Orange peel.
- Silicones.

• Dust specks and dirt

The most common defect is dust falling on the model during painting or while it is still wet. In the majority of environments, there are quite a lot of dust specks suspended in the air. A quick solution is to spray water all around before painting to saturate and make these specks drop to the floor. It is also advisable to use cloths that do not shed fuzz or fibres, so-called nap free material. Finally, buying the same sort of cover as that used by professional vehicle painters is also advisable.

If a dust speck is detected on the paint, it is best to leave it there until the paint is completely dry. Do not attempt to remove it, say, with a needle, as there is an easy -although laborious- solution.

• Runs

A run is where the applied paint, for one reason or another, usually too much paint, has formed into a tear-like blob and sagged down the part that is being painted. These are just as common on lacquered surfaces as painted ones.

They can be caused by a number of things, spraying too slowly, too close or using too much pressure. Another cause can be too low a temperature inside in the room where the model is being painted. It is always advisable to work in an environment above 20°C.

While these are not common flaws for experienced modellers, it is always best to give a model an extra coat than trying to do the job in one go.

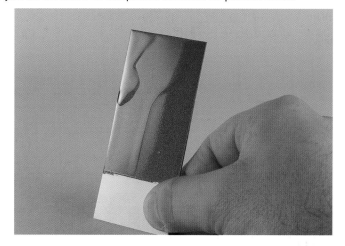

Sagging caused by using too much paint or lacquer. In this case, it was done on a plastic test card. These cards are useful for testing the mixture and paint colour and for getting used to particular paints used in airbrushes or spray guns.

• Orange peel

It is so named because the texture is like that of orange peel. In fact, it is caused by lack of elasticity by spraying to close to the model or the paint is too viscous.

Note how lacquer has not properly extended and there is no evenness: this is the typical orange peel defect.

• Silicones

Silicones are cavities similar to craters. Their cause is not easy to determine; usually it is the result of dirt, greasy hands, oil from the compressor sprayed through the airbrush or even spray products such as deodorants, perfumes, aftershave etc.

Before spraying paint or lacquers it is imperative, as stated in Section 16, to wash or degrease parts using a suitable product. Never use nitro cellulose or universal solvent as these separate paint. Soapy water is a near perfect solution for this job.

There is also a product called anti-silicones, used by professional body shops but this is not really necessary for modellers. If all the parts are cleaned properly and touching them with bare hands is avoided, there should be no problem.

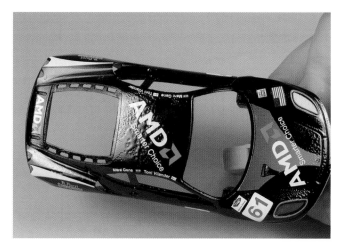

Note how the lacquer does not cover properly. This defect is caused by grease or other foreign agents that 'repel' lacquer or paint. To check for the cause, lacquer another spare part under the same environmental conditions and if the flaw doesn't appear, it means that the problem resides on the actual piece.

17.3 How to correct flaws?

All the above problems can be treated in the same way, except silicones, and these will be dealt with separately.
Here is one example that is applicable to most cases: how to remove a large dust speck.
Basically, the solution is the gradual use of ever-finer grade abrasive papers. While it is a simple task, it is tedious. The papers used are special purpose ones that are easily available on the market.

Finishing paper available in small
sheets or plastic frames.

The complete process.
First, mask off the area with masking tape to protect the
remainder of the part. Rub gently with a 1200grade paper until
the surface is completely smooth and flat.

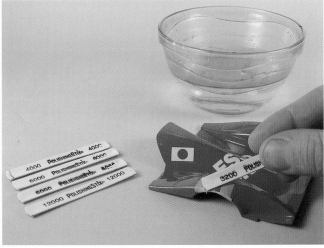

All that remains now is to recover the gloss finish. To do this,
continue to rub down, this time using a 3200 grade paper.

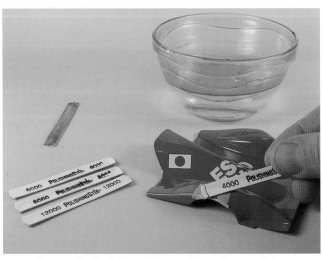

Then, with Wet'n'Dry 4000 grade, continue rubbing.

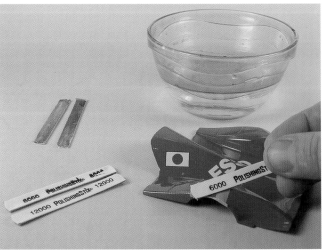

Then, with Wet'n'Dry 6000 grade, continue rubbing.

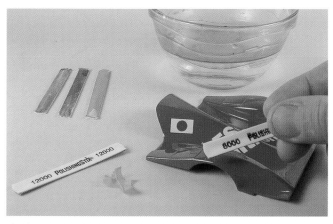

Next, remove the masking tape and continue rubbing with 8000 grade Wet 'n' Dry paper. You will notice that the gloss is beginning to re-emerge.

Rubbing with Wet 'n' Dry paper is completed using a 12000 grade paper. Gloss is almost total by now.

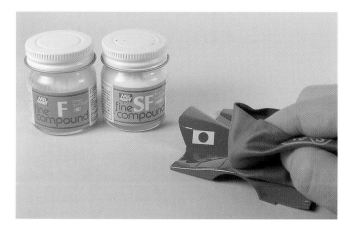

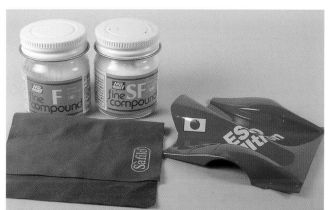

The final touch is to give the area a very fine polishing applied with a glass cleaning cloth until the gloss is the same over the whole piece.

As stated earlier, all flaws are solved using the same method, except silicones that require sandpapering over the whole piece using 1200, 1500 or 2000 and water; then degreasing or washing again and, finally, re-painting or re-lacquering.

18. SHADING AN EFFECT ON CARBON FIBRE

As is widely known, carbon fibre is a material increasingly used in vehicle manufacture and specially in racing examples. Carbon fibre has a high gloss due to its resin component, although time and temperature tend to reduce this over time. These effects can also be reproduced on a model.

18.1 How can these effects be reproduced on carbon fibre?

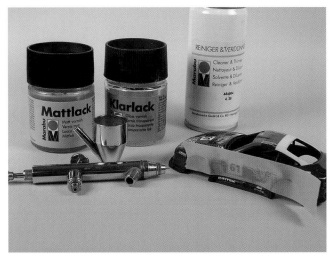

After the carbon fibre decal has been applied, apply a coat of matt varnish directly or mix a little gloss and matt varnish together to get a more realistic, satin tone, thus giving it a different appearance from the overall tone of the bodywork.

A technique that, perhaps, requires some extra effort, but giving a more realistic finish consists of accentuating the glossiness of the car industry lacquer.

On the part that was covered earlier with the carbon fibre decal, car lacquer was applied and left to dry for several days.

Then, using 3200, 3600 or 4000 Wet 'n' Dry paper, erase all the gloss until a flat, perfectly even finish is obtained.

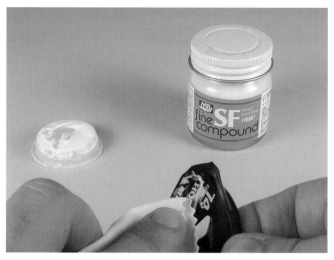

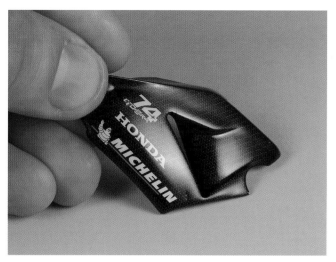

Using polishing paste, rub the surface with a glass cleaning cloth until some gloss returns, but never as much as previously. This treatment will result in a finish of great realism that contrast nicely with brightness of the bodywork.

A higher gloss can be obtained by simply finish polishing with either 6000 or 8000 Wet 'n' Dry paper or 2000 Wet 'n' Dry followed by polishing paste.

Note how this Ducati GP mudguard has been treated in this way to achieve a very realistic finish.

19. DOORS AND WINDOW FRAMES

19.1 Introduction

This job is undertaken after lacquering the bodywork and accomplished using paint that allows for cleaning, retouching and even removal. Of course, for this job, the airbrush is the perfect tool. A brush could also be used, but it would have to be done with great skill to get an even finish. And, let's face it, using the airbrush is both easier and gives the best result.

The following process shows how to paint door and window surrounds. However, the same process could be used to paint other similar components such as roof and door seals, bodywork, rubber joints and so on.

19.2 What is the process for painting door and window frames?

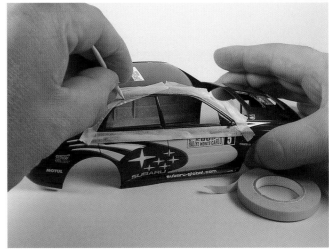

First the whole outline must be masked off with adhesive tape. Around difficult areas the tip of a toothpick is very useful.

A new scalpel blade (otherwise the cut will be not sharp enough) is used to trim the spare masking tape without exerting any pressure.

After the outlines are masked and the rest of the bodywork protected, apply the black acrylic paint. This has low adherence that allows for any eventual removal. Any over-painting can be easily, and gently removed with the point of a toothpick.

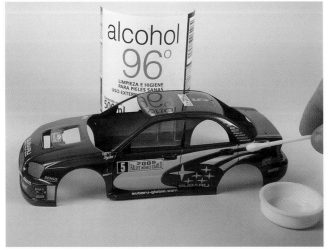

Any over-painting and residue can be cleaned off with a cotton bud soaked in alcohol or gently rubbed off with a toothpick.

20. ATTACHING RIVETS AND OTHER ACCESSORIES TO THE BODYWORK

Complementary items, including aerials, rivets or catches are small additions that add that extra touch of realism to models. While they are a small investment in terms of time and effort, their impact is huge in terms of end result.

A selection of complementary items.

20.1 Fixing these complementary items

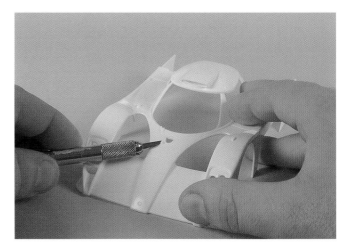

The first thing to do is identify, mark and prepare the surface.

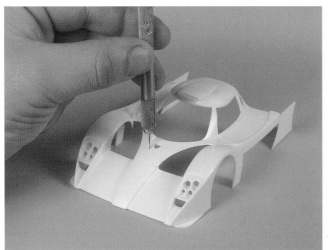

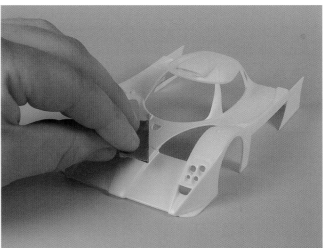

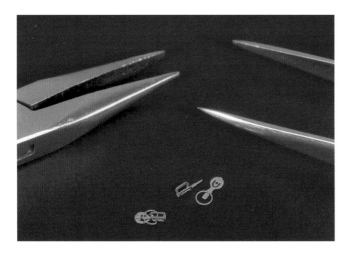

A good quality tool is required for accurate bending. It should be glued like all the other complementary items in earlier sections.

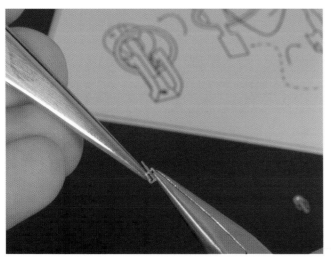

20.2 How to make safety belts?

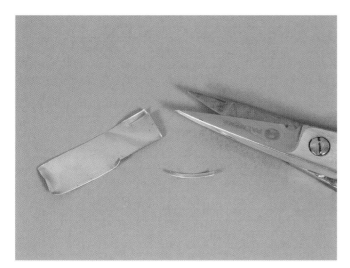
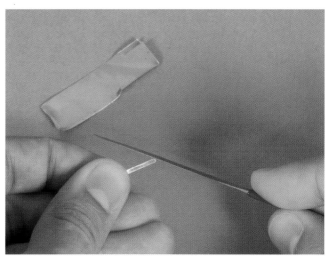

Cut out some thin metal strips and shape them with a file.

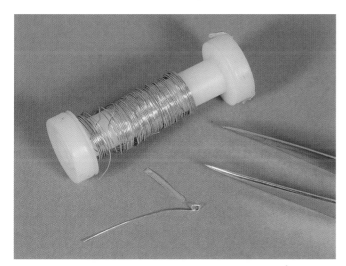

The buckles can be made from wire, using tweezes and pliers.

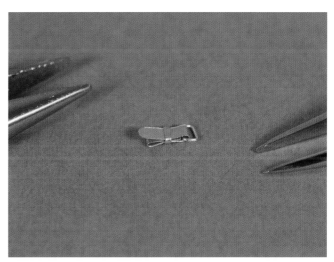

The metal strips are bent in the same way.

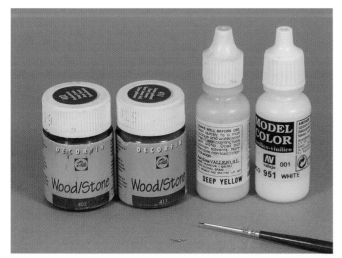

The belt is painted in different shades of brown. The depth of colour will increase if the base colour used is either yellow or white.

20.3 How to assemble rivets and aerials?

Sometimes a coat of lacquer may clog the holes drilled earlier for the rivets. If so, these must be re-opened or enlarged.

Rivets are fitted with tweezers.

Rivets are fitted with the help of a non-metallic element.

Aerial holders can be made in the same way.

20.4 How to make aerials?

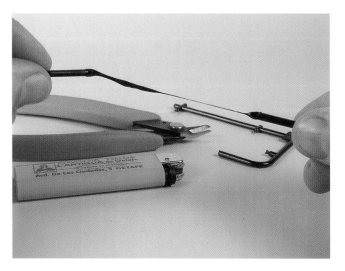

While there are stock aerials, including fine steel rod, the old technique of stretched plastic sprue is still perfectly adequate. This procedure consists of heating a length of plastic rod from the kit's sprues until it is soft enough as to be gently stretched by pulling it from both ends until it reaches the desired thickness.
Simple, cheap and, surprisingly, strong!

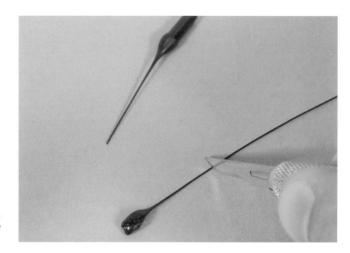

The diameter is fixed according to requirements and always maintaining the correct scale. The tip is then sharpened and the aerial painted if required.

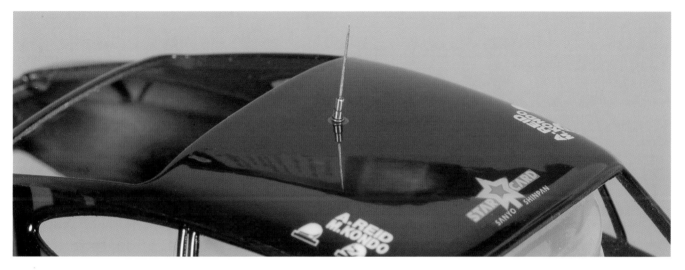

21. HOW TO ASSEMBLE WINDOWS, LIGHTS, INDICATORS AND PLASTIC LIGHTS

Handling transparent parts is a very delicate modelling operation, as any scratch or flaw will be instantly noticeable. Little by little, kit manufacturers are improving transparencies and making their assembly more precise. They are now even supplying coloured rear indicators.

21.1 How to eliminate flaws in transparent plastic parts?

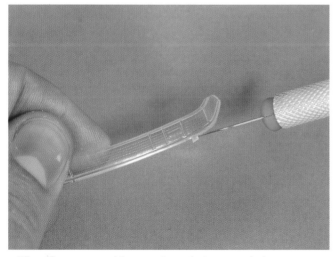

When flaws or mould seams have to be erased always use a new scalpel blade as they will help to make a much better job.

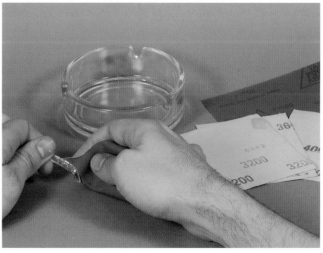

A sandpapered transparency has a whitish colour. Full transparency can be restored by successive use of finer sandpapers (3200 to 1200).

21.2 How to paint transparent parts?

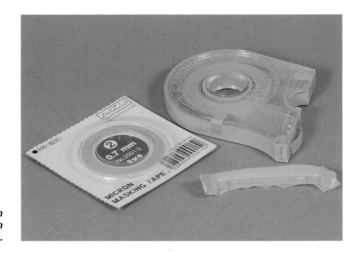

To get a uniform finish, the best way is to paint each part from the inside. If required, the colours can be separated with masking tape.

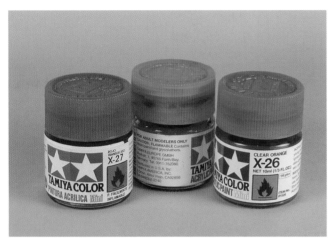

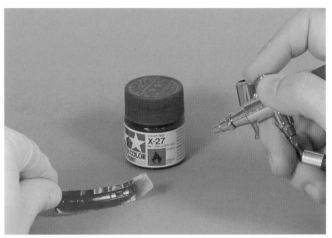

Coloured transparent paints are perfect for these processes.

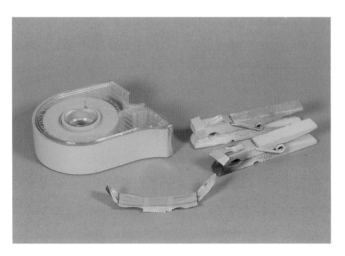

If required, change the colour and re-mask.

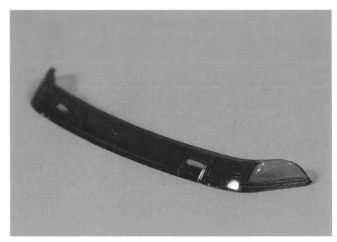

21.3 How to prepare reflectors in lights and indicators?

To get a deep metallic effect, a piece of metallic adhesive tape can be used.

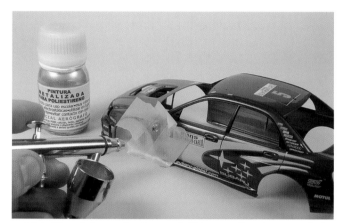 

Metallic paint can also be used. If lacquer has been applied earlier, eliminate any surplus with a cotton bud soaked in alcohol.

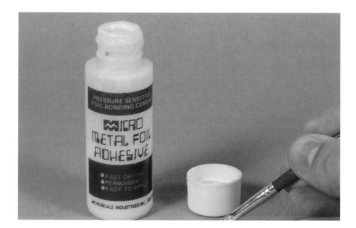 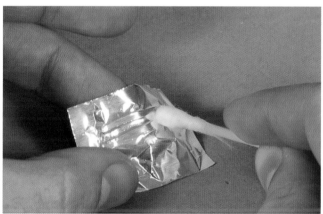

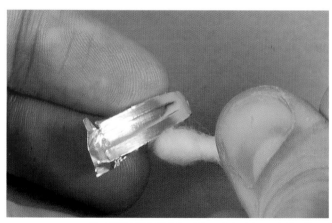 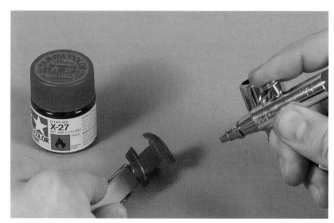

If a light is not transparent or has a defective finish, the problem can be put right by using a piece of metallic adhesive tape and painting it with transparent colours.

21.4 How to glue transparent parts?

Many glues produce gases that can damage transparent plastics. For this reason, white PVA glue or special purpose glue designed for this type of material should be used.

To make the application easier, first dilute the glue and apply it with a brush.

Use a small piece of Blu-Tack to correctly position the light before gluing.

The part is then held with a small stick and the putty removed.

Another method -if it is needed- to integrate the lamp with the body work is to use lacquer as the adhesive medium thus maintaining a uniform gloss with the rest of the bodywork. However, it should be noted that lacquer attacks transparent plastics. For this reason, some protective and transparent priming must first be applied.

The final result after applying lacquer.

21.5 How to make patterns for windows?

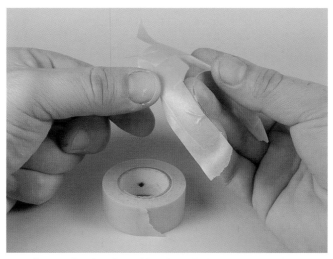

Use professional masking tape that leaves no residue.

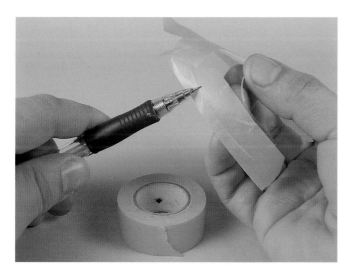

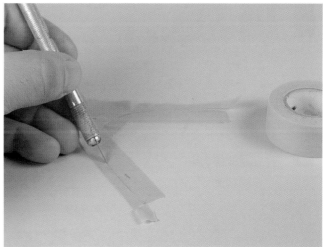

Outline with a pencil and then cut.

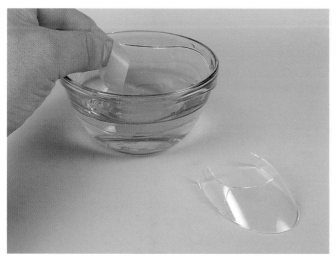

*The mask is soaked to soften the adhesive
and to make the application much easier*

*Once dry, the adhesive
strength is restored.*

With the pattern completed, the colour is applied with an airbrush.

The final result.

22. ASSEMBLING ACETATE LIGHTS AND WINDOWS

22.1 Introduction

Many models come supplied with acetate sheet (a type of PVC plastic) to be used for lights, windshields and windows. The smaller 1/43 scale models are rather difficult to deal with when using this material. For this reason, here are some hints for working with models of this scale.

Before beginning, it should be noted that, unlike plastic transparencies, lacquer does not damage acetate sheet. From our point of view, completing the integration of lights and windows in this scale is achieved better by using lacquer.

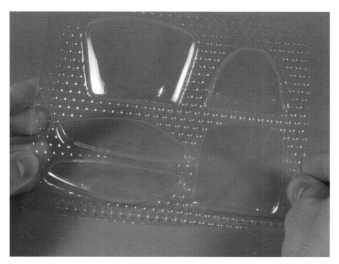

Pre-formed acetate sheet included with some kits.

22.2 How to assemble acetate lights?

The first step is to mark, with a felt-tip pen, on the part so you have a reference of where it is to be assembled.

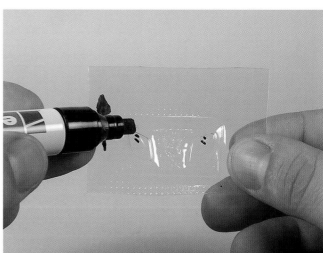

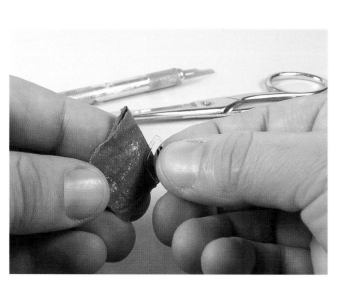

The part is then cut from the acetate sheet. At this juncture, be careful and cut out the part slightly larger than required to allow for any eventual adjustments that cannot be implemented if the piece is trimmed to the exact size.
The edges of the part should be sandpapered with a medium grade paper. This should be carried out at a right angle to the edges of the part to avoid any surface damage.

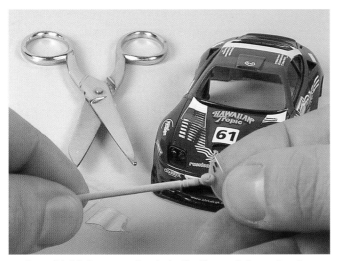

A good trick to remember is to fix the acetate part onto a toothpick with a little Blu-Tack so that checks can be made while sandpapering to ensure you don't remove too much and to ensure a good fit.

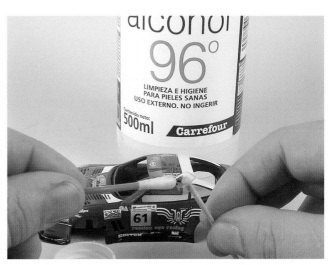

Once the part has been measured and assembled, clean the inner side with a cotton bud dipped in alcohol.

When the part is ready, glue it in with white PVA glue (polyvinyl acetates), this becomes transparent when dry.

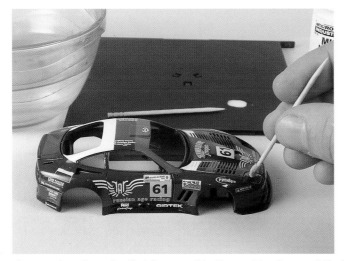

Once again using a toothpick, assemble the part in place and fix it with adhesive tape until the glue is completely dry. It then only remains to remove the tape, while holding the part in place with another toothpick to prevent it coming loose. Finally, clean the light and surrounding area with alcohol.

22.3 How to work with acetate windows before gluing?

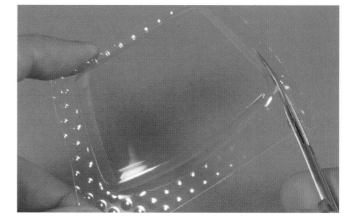

Trimming is similar to the earlier case. But, as this time the part is bigger, the work will be that much easier.

The part is placed in position and the surplus marked with a felt pen.

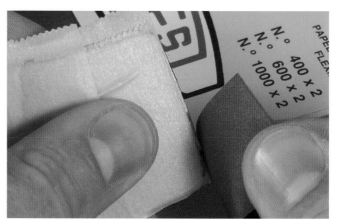

The part is masked with tape to protect if from possible mistakes and the remaining material sandpapered.

22.4 How to glue acetate windows?

This time let us proceed with a side window. First, place it in position before gluing and hold it with adhesive tape.

Once the part is positioned correctly, proceed to glue it. The first thing to do is remove the tape from one side using two toothpicks: one to hold the part and the other to apply the glue (in this case, cyanoacrilate, superglue). When handling large parts that have to be fixed to curved surfaces, it is best to use instant superglue. However, it should be noted that this glue should be handled with great care, using it in tiny amounts and applying it perpendicularly to the part on just a few points and not all around the edge.

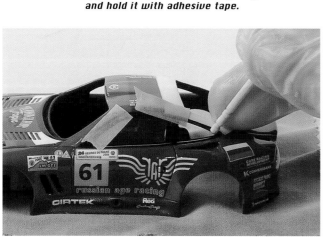

Immediately after the glue has been applied, apply a little pressure with the other end of the toothpick for a few seconds. Finally, check that the window has successfully glued all round.

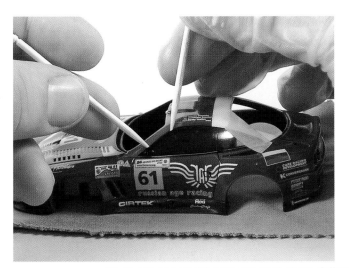 

When one end of the part has been fixed, follow the same procedure for the remaining points.
White glue could, of course, also be used for this operation. However, we have discovered that, sometimes
it ages and the part comes unglued. According to our experience, superglue is the best gluing medium for this job.

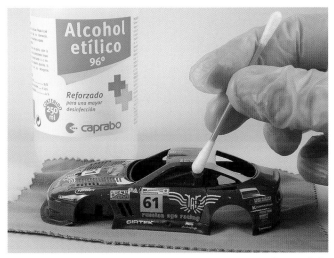

The final step, as usual, is to carefully clean off all fingerprints
and other marks with alcohol.

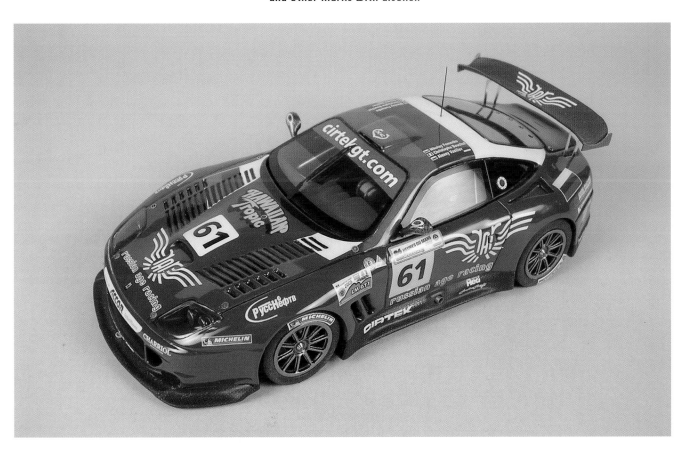

23. WHEELS AND TYRES

First, tyres should be painted to represent normal wear and tear and the manufacturer's logos should be added. Wheels should not be painted in exactly the same shade, but given them subtle differences and then add some extra details as a final touch.

23.1 How to prepare and paint tyres?

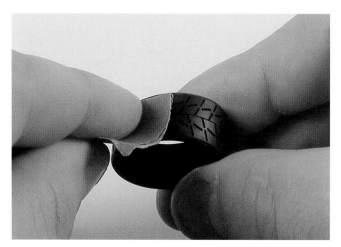 

The central molding line around the tyre is easily eliminated using P400 grade sandpaper and Scotch Brite.

 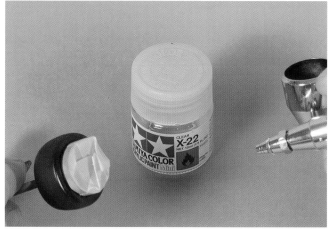

Gloss varnish is then applied with either a brush or airbrush. Once dry, the manufacturer's lettering can be applied.

 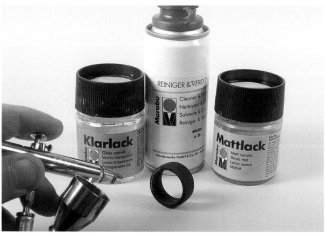

Decals are applied as explained in earlier chapters. Extra ones for tyres have to be outlined, placed in the correct position, and moistened with a water-soaked brush. After a few moments, the backing sheet can be removed with tweezers.

An overall coat of satin or matt varnish is then applied to cover any remaining gloss varnish.

There are available, as an after-market item, specific patterns of tyre logos in the form of photo-etched stencils that can be used to airbrush the logos onto the tyres.

23.2 How to prepare and paint wheels?

Basically, there are three types of wheels: wheels painted with standard paint, lacquered wheels and alloy wheels.

First, give them a coat of gloss varnish.

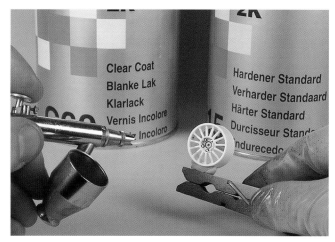

The wheels can be lacquered over a base acrylic or enamel colour.
The lacquer should be applied after any decals, or other effects have been completed.

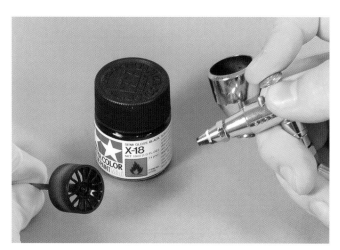

When painting an alloy wheel, first give them a coat of gloss black. Following that, a coat of the chosen
metallic paint can be applied. In this way, the colour, shape and tone will be enhanced.

23.3 Introducing some extra effects on wheels

Without doubt, depending on the vehicle and its environment, some extra effects can always be added to make them
both stand out and enhance their realism.

On a gold wheel, a darker, metallic colour
is subtly airbrushed at low pressure.

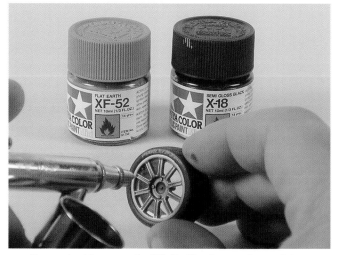

The central boss can be "dirtied" using a colour mixture
matching that of the environment you wish to portray. This one
belongs to a Subaru WRC 05 as driven
in the 2005 Monte Carlo Rally. In this particular case,
the vehicle is depicted at the beginning of the event.

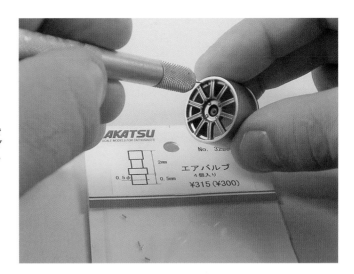

Tyre valves can be scratchbuilt and fitted for that extra touch of realism.

Bolt heads can be made from photo-etched rivets, painted separately and, when dry, glued on with PVA wooden glue.

24. DISC BRAKES

Disc brakes are made from steel, although carbon discs can also be found on racing vehicles. Accordingly, we should be prepared to simulate these two materials in respect of the effects of wear and tear.
In addition, a choice of photo etched kits are available on the market for improving or even replacing the brakes.

24.1 How to make carbon discs?

The texture of carbon discs can be represented using a mixture of black and a highly pigmented, rather glossy metallic grey, depending on the amount of wear and tear required.

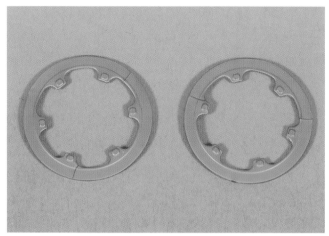

*Note the disc and stub axle
integrated on the same part.*

*The whole part is painted with a metallic chrome colour,
identical to the one on the rivets joining both parts.*

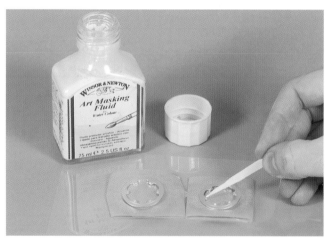

*Rivets covered with
liquid mask.*

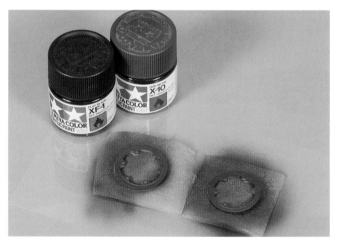

*Painted with a mixture of black
and a dark metallic colour.*

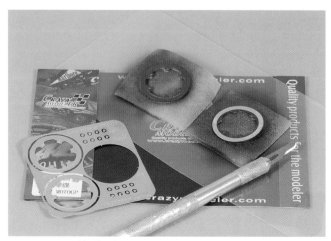

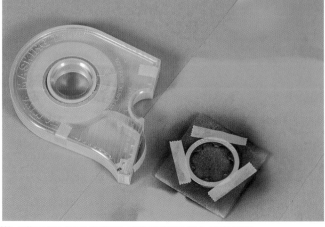

Stock photo etched patterns can be used and fixed with adhesive tape before airbrushing the stub axle.

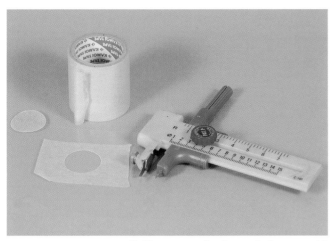 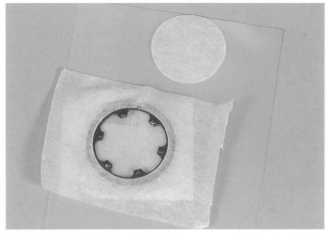

Patterns can also be made from masking tape with the help of a cutting compass.

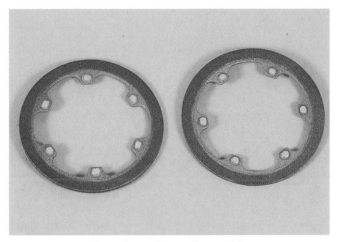

*The end result once the masking
has been removed.*

24.2 How to make a carbon disc with photo etch?

Photo etching accessories for disc brakes.

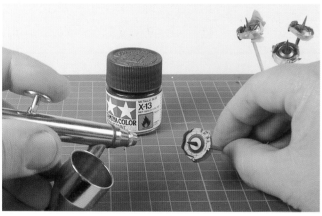

Discs are prepared by first erasing any flaws.

Another example of colours used for painting carbon discs.

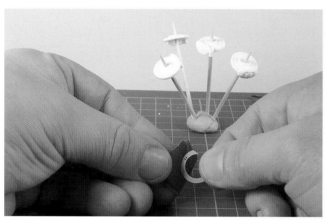

The stub axle painted.

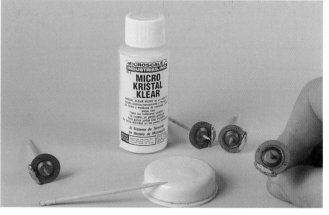

Photo etched discs glued onto the stub axle.

24.2 How to make steel disc brakes?

These can be painted or the disc brake made from photo etching that requires no paint.

Paint them with gloss black to enhance the final metallic finish.

24.4 How to simulate the effects of wear and tear?

Add some very subtle effects extremely carefully. Making sure that scale is maintained.

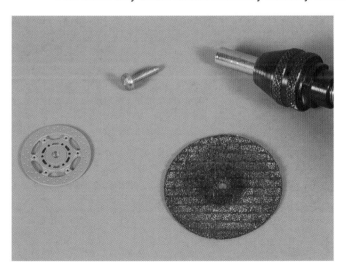

The disc is fitted into a mini drill chuck, turned and filed. The final polishing is done with medium grade sandpaper.

With disc still fitted into the drill chuck, use a medium grade sandpaper disc surface to lightly 'scratch' the disc's surface to simulate wear and tear.

25. ENGINES

The immense variety of materials that go into making an engine forces us to use a number of different painting techniques and effects. This diversity will go a long way in making the engine a showpiece in itself. On the market today are many types of modelling paints that are able to represent very effectively all these materials. However, it is still necessary to, now and again, mix metallic and solid colours, use decals to simulate carbon fibre, and some other tricks to attain a desired texture or finish.

25.1 How to paint the crankcase, cylinder heads and the general parts of the engine?

Some engine parts, depending on materials they are made of, can be a solid or metallic colour.

Renault RE 20 engine

• Solid colours

More often than not, a number of colours have to be mixed to get a desired shade.

• Metallic colours

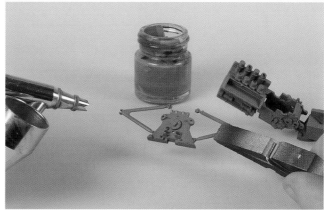

A huge range of metallic colours are available: aluminium, magnesium, steel, copper, gold, chrome, etc.

To enliven some metal tones, it is first necessary to apply a base colour; gloss or satin black or even a shade of red, dependent on the effect we are trying to achieve.

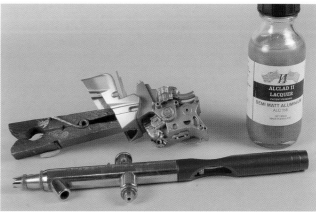

The correct metal colour is applied. Then, another enhancing colour is added so as to avoid at all costs a monochromatic finish.

• Effects

An element of showiness can be added with the addition of different oil tones using some specific colours that are related to the base colour.

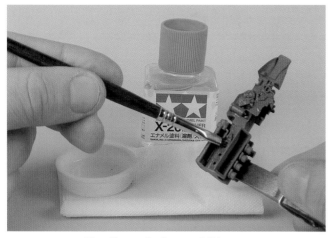

Give it a coat of enamel thinners.

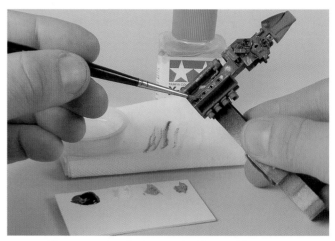

Tiny amounts of oil are added in specific places.

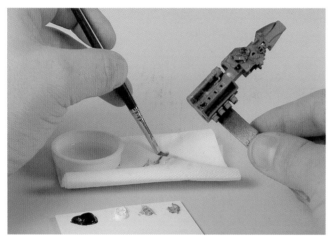

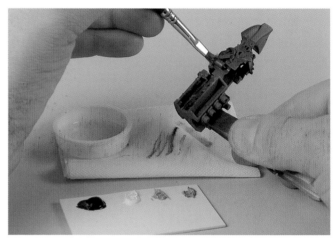

A thinner-soaked brush is used to spread the pigments, maintaining the same direction so that they blend together. However, make sure to avoid a blurred effect.

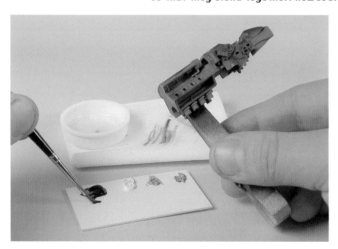

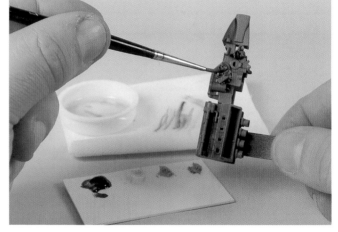

Black oil may be used on some particular areas.

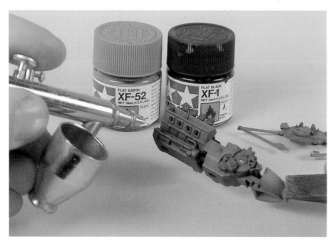

The airbrush can also be used after mixing some highly diluted colours.

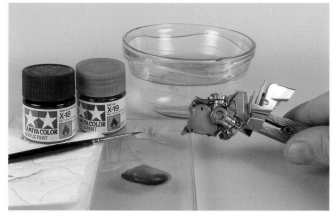

A 'wash' is a technique whereby a lot of water or thinner is added to a colour (often a dark one) and then this painted, using a fine brush, in such a way that the paint flows around the intricate parts making the shape stand out that much more. Subtlety is the watchword when using this technique. It is much better to repeat the process a number of times rather than spoiling the whole model by over-applying the mixture in one go.

'Dry Brushing' is a technique used to enhance the paint job by emphasizing all the high points of a particular part. A lighter colour than the base is chosen, usually taking the base colour and adding a lighter colour to it there by maintaining a homogenous whole. A flat brush is then loaded with the mixture and then most of it is removed onto a piece of clean paper or nap-free rag until the brush is almost dry.

With gentle, but lively, regular strokes, rub the brush over the whole of the piece you want to highlight, especially around the sharp edges. Soon, you will notice how the shapes begin to stand out.

On left side can be seen the result of painting with oils (gear box) while, on the right, can be seen the work done with the airbrush to simulate the effects of temperature.

Washes and dry brush treatments were used in both cases.

25.2 How to paint exhausts?

Metallic paint is used with the effects of heat, wear, dirt, etc., added later

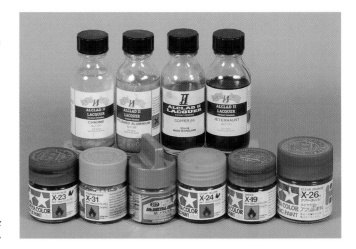

The effects were done using metallic paints and clear varnishes.

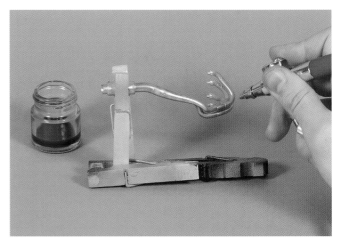

Highly diluted transparent shades were applied all round, especially on bends and welds. For this, several colours, such as yellows and greens, were mixed.

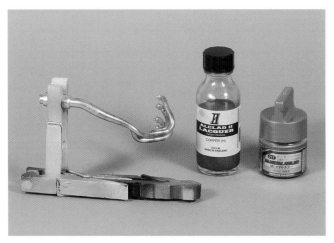

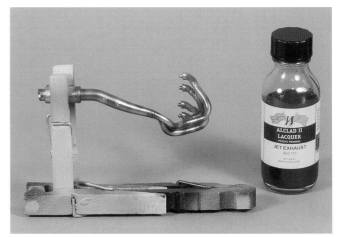

Metallic tones were used on more prominent points.

Smoke colours can be also applied for enhancing different points.

The completed appearance of a motorcycle exhaust.

Exhaust soot can be simulated with dark, dirty and flat colours obtained by mixing highly diluted blacks, greys and browns and then airbrushed on the required areas.

25.3 How to paint different colours on small parts?

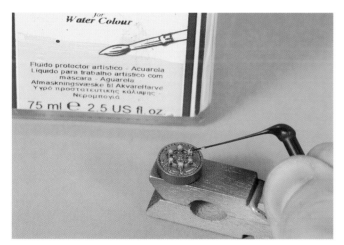

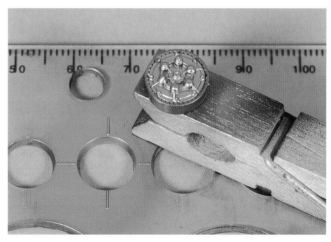

First, airbrush a base colour and then mask off the painted area with tape.
Once the base colour is dry, the next colour can be airbrushed. Finally, remove the masking tape and, as a last touch, added some selective washes.

25.4 How to hide bolts?

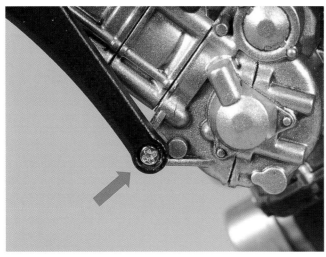

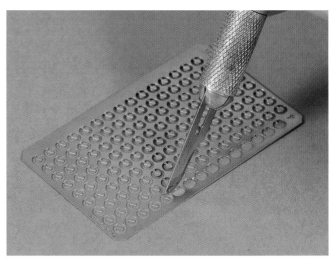

A number of kits, especially motorcycles, quite often have over-scale bolt heads showing (these are used to fix the bodywork or engine).

Photo-etched scale bolts can be used or, alternatively, reverse them.

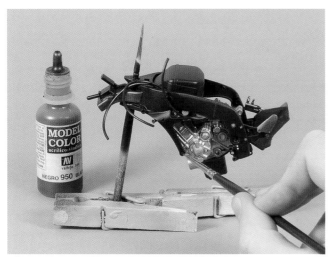

The part is glued and painted in the correct colour.

25.5 How to improve carburettor intake trumpets?

Protective mesh grills will have to be made to fit the top of the intake trumpets.

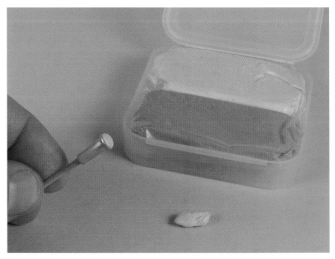

As these grills are half-spherical and to make them it is necessary to make a mould from putty.

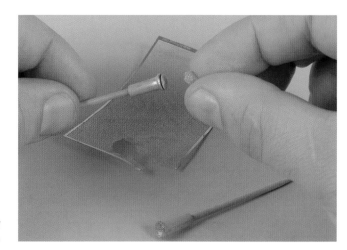

Cut the mesh as required and
shape it over the mould.

Painting and adding effects.

25.6 What types of materials can be used to simulate cables and tubing?

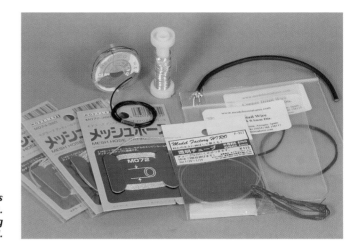

Cables and transparent or textured hoses are available from many hobby shops. However, electrical wire, tin reels, fishing line, etc. can also be used.

Assembling cables and tubing. Always maintain the correct scale.

25.7 Making brackets for tubing and sleeves?

These can be made from fine line, tying and gluing it on the reverse so it is not visible.

Adhesive metallic sheet is also available in most modelling shops and this can be also used. The 'silver' paper wrapping in a cigarette packet also comes in useful.

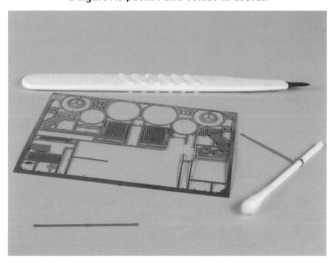

Another handy item are the spare frames from photo-etched parts: they are flexible and can be easily cut to the required width.

26. MODELLING INTERIORS

This is, perhaps, one of the least rewarding jobs, as most vehicles are closed and, consequently, hidden from the observers' eye to some extent. For this reason, some modellers do not give it the attention it deserves. Others, on the other hand, find satisfaction in knowing a full work has been developed and interiors fully modelled.

26.1 How to paint sport seats?

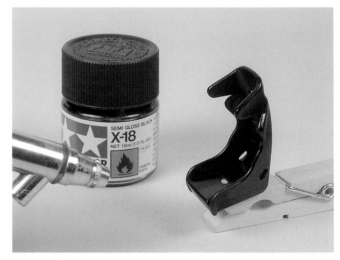

Begin by airbrushing the seat in a gloss colour.

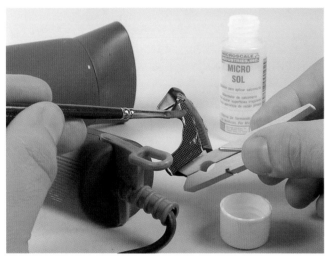
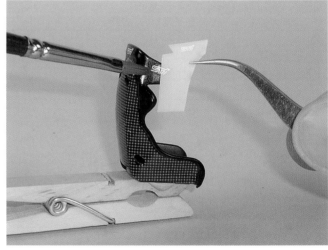

If the seat requires, apply the manufacturer's decals on the rear to simulate Kevlar or carbon fibre.

Gloss varnish or lacquer can be applied to the seat back to enhance different points or textures.

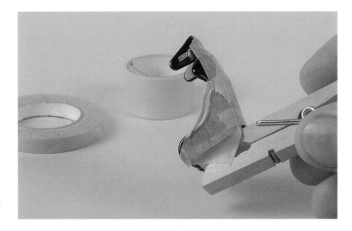

Using adhesive masking tape to mask before further treatment with matt varnish.

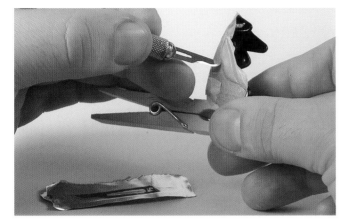

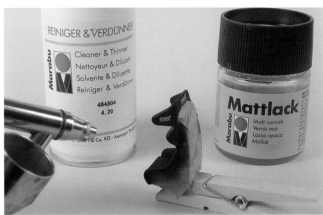

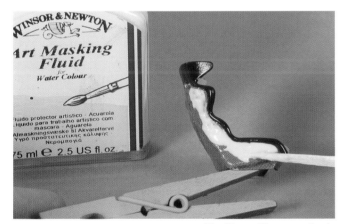

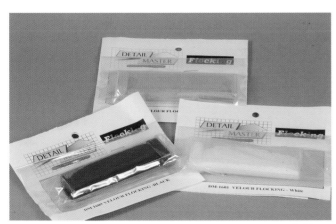

Liquid masking can also be used to get the same effect.

26.2 How make textured sports seats?

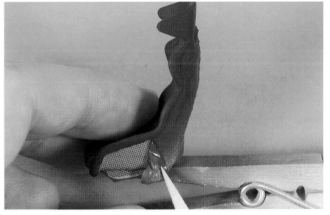

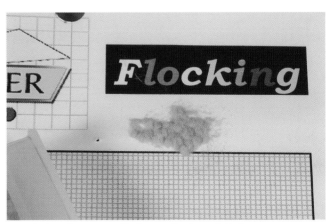

Fabric powder in several colours is available on the market and, once applied, can also be painted.

107

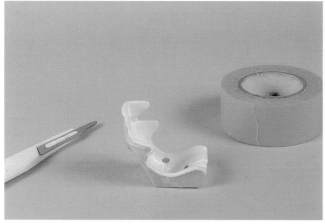

Areas not to be textured are masked.

Spray glue as used in the upholstery trade was used.

Pour the fabric powder into a container.

The whole seat is covered with the powder that, in its turn, will be glued to it.

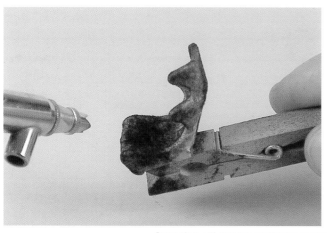

Once dry, all excess material is removed with air pressure and a brush.

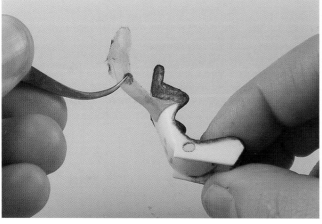

The masking tape is removed to treat the rear of the seat.

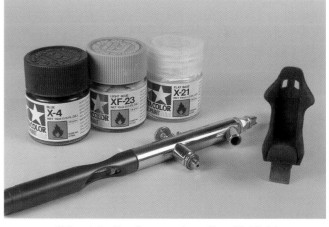

Airbrush in the chosen colour, then highlight using a lighter version of the base colour.

26.3 How to make safety belts or riggings

Some kits are supplied with decals that simulate riggings, or they are carved on the seats or have flat –non textured- straps. It is best to disregard all these solutions and instead replace them with some textured fabrics in scale.

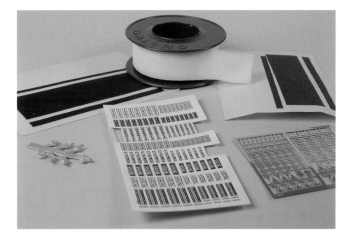

Use sticking plaster or special stock strips.

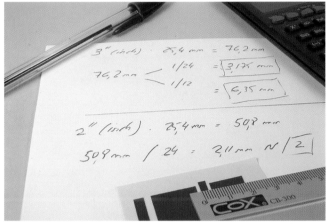

Whatever is used, make sure they are in scale. This is an example of how to calculate the scale width for any given length: in this case, 1/24 and 1/12.

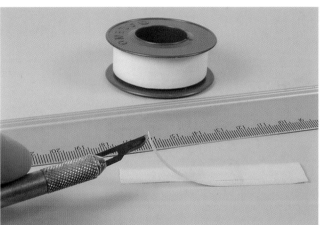

Use a craft knife to cut the plaster before painting.

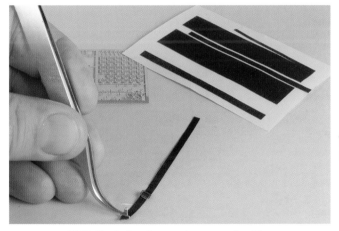

With the help of some tweezers buckles can be moved till get the correct position.

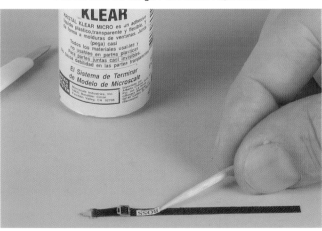

The rigging manufacturer's logo is glued with white glue onto the rigging.

26.4 How to paint a steering wheel?

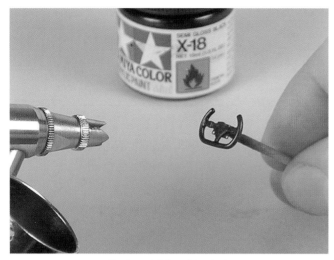

First, paint it satin black.

To represent suede, apply flat black to the steering wheel and give it three highlights by mixing black with any other colour; in this instance, pink as the final shade should be violet.

As a complementary part of the steering wheel, add the control column stalks using stock photo etched parts from other kits.

26.5 How to improve dashboards?

Often, kits come supplied with a flat decal for the dashboard. This cries out for a bit of superdetailing.

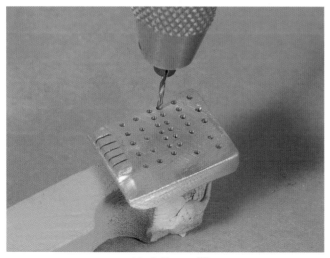

Mark the position of the switches.

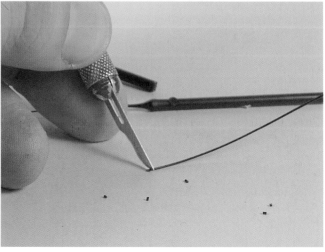

Switches can be made from heat stretched plastic cut to the correct length.

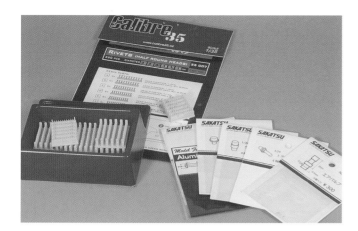

Stock complements can also be used.

26.6 How to make a pedal stand?

It is always possible to introduce some simple improvements easily. This next example can be extended to many other cases.

In this case, use a readily available 0.3mm thick plastic card.

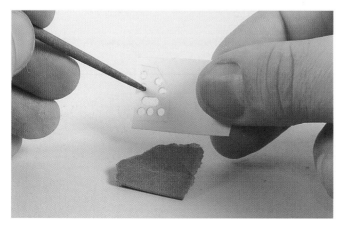

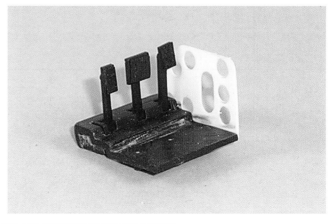

After drawing it onto the Plasticard, use bits and files to get clean holes.

26.7 How to make thermic fabrics?

 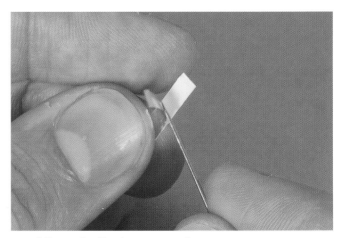

Metallic adhesive tape is cut to measure and the protective tape removed.

 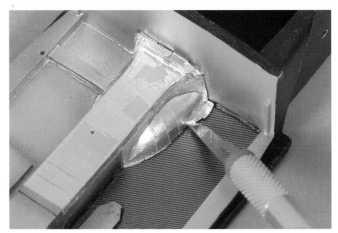

This type of paper fits perfectly with the help of a cotton bud. Any surplus is removed with a knife.

Stock textured papers are also available or even the paper from cigarette packets can be used.

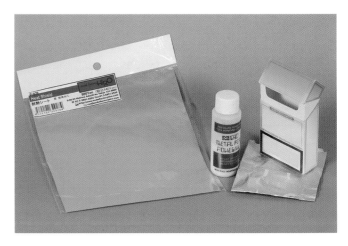

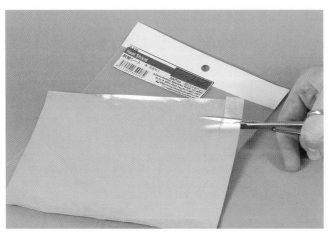 

26.8 How to make electrical connectors?

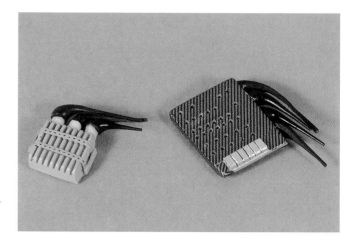

Heat stretched plastic sprue is a simple, effective method for making electrical connectors. Take advantage of the typical conical shape of stretched plastic rod ends.

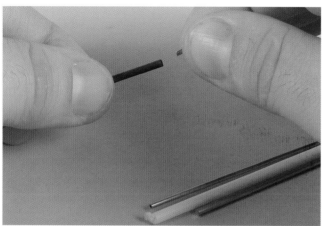

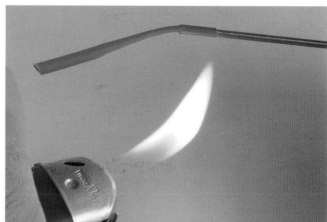

Another way to make connectors for electronic switchboards is by cutting a tube to measure and then place it inside a heat-retractile pipe (shrinks when heated) that is readily available in specialized shops.

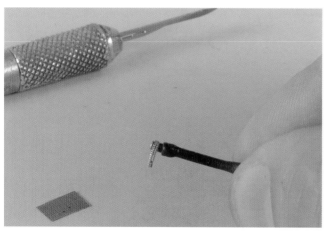

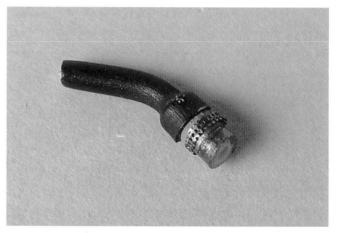

Roll a spare photo etched strip onto the treated tube to represent the connector lock.

26.9 How to make a safety cage?

In this example, a roll cage will be constructed after taking the measurements from the original kit-supplied item that has been discarded.

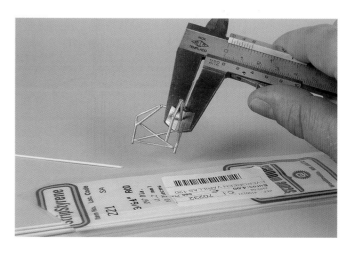

The first step is to select the correct diameter of plastic tubing, ensuring that it is the correct scale.

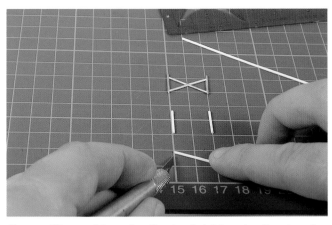

Use a cutting mat to make all cuts at right angles thus insuring that all the parts will be problem free during assembly.

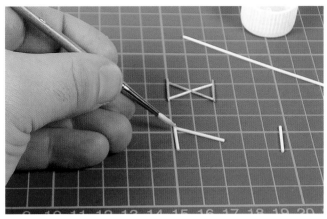

The parts are glued together using either universal solvent, modelling cement or cyanoacrilate.

Tin solder is used to heat the tubes before bending them, taking care not to touch the part or apply excessive heat, otherwise the shape could be damaged. Simply twist the tube until it bends. To know exactly where the bending point is, just mark it with a felt pen.

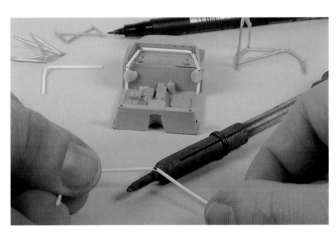

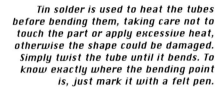

Once the main parts are ready, assemble them inside the car interior to insure that all the measurements are correct.

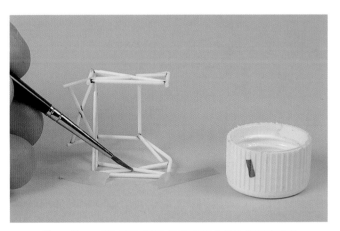

Once the main structure is finished, the remainder of the parts can be fitted before final assembly.

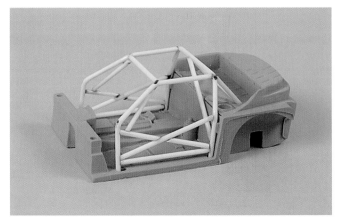

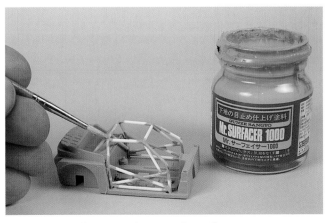

Once the cage has been assembled, liquid putty is applied to all the seams to conceal any flaw.

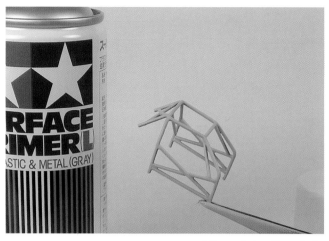

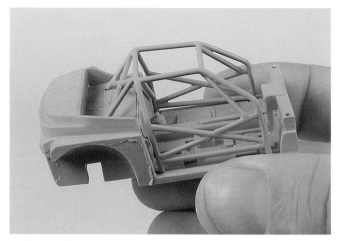

After priming the whole piece, the work is complete.

27. MAKING MOULDS AND CASTING RESIN PARTS

27.1 Introduction

Sometimes, it is necessary to introduce modifications to some pieces and even cast some copies. Improving original parts or using resin copies to replace heavier white metal parts are common. Consequently, this section is dedicated to the creation of simple -and more complex- moulds so it is necessary to learn a little about how to handle the various materials used in the moulding trade.

Due to the fact that many products used in moulding are toxic, reading the manufacturer's instructions and labelling is strongly recommended for the sake of personal safety.

27.2 What is a mould intended for?

Moulds are used to replicate a given piece. Usually silicone moulds deteriorate after around 20 castings.

27.3 What materials do I need?

A mould requires silicone and a catalyser, while resin and its respective catalyser will be used for the actual casting. All these items are available from specialised shops. We will not recommend any brand in particular. There are many manufactures producing good quality materials and the choice will usually rest on the availability, product knowledge, brand, etc.

• What materials are used for making the mould?

Silicone and its catalyser.

Plasticard is used to box or plank the proposed mould, so a steel rule, craft knife, pencil, etc., are required.

Polyurethane resin and its catalyser.

27.4 How to make simple moulds?

• By building boxes or forms

Plasticard is used, with the help of a steel rule and a craft knife, to build a container large enough as to hold the part we want to replicate.

It is not necessary to cut the planks apart with the cutter; just mark them and slight hand pressure will force them apart.

The part is glued to a plastic base with super glue. Positioning the part is a crucial step as, once the mould is completed, this base will be the feeder; that is, it is the point through which resin will be poured.

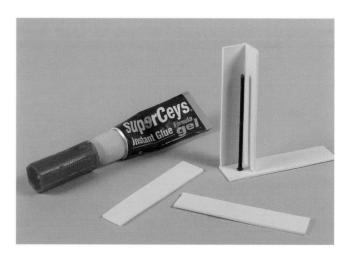

The container is completed by gluing plastic planks together (superglue).
It should be noted, silicone is a liquid and will tend to leak through the mould seams. For this reason, all seams should be sealed with diluted white PVA glue (polyvinyl acetate) applied with an old brush.

The silicone must be thoroughly stirred with a rod before pouring the predetermined amount into a container.

Silicone cures by the action of a specific manufacturer-supplied catalyser. In this particular case, a 5% catalyser is added to the silicone and 24 hours will be needed before the curing process is completed for a mould suited with the correct mechanical and chemical features. However, that said, and according to our own experience, a 30 minute, fast drying, can be obtained by using a 30% catalyser mixture.
The resulting mould has been found to be more than adequate for successive castings.

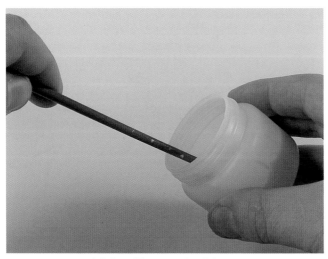

Mixing silicone and catalyser.

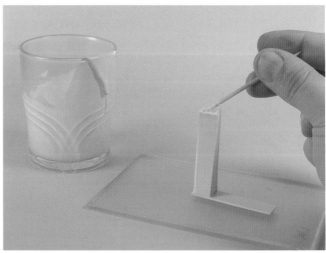

By slowly pouring the mixture into the container allow bubbles to emerge. Once the container has been filled, 'puncture' the silicone with a toothpick or a pin to allow the trapped air to escape.

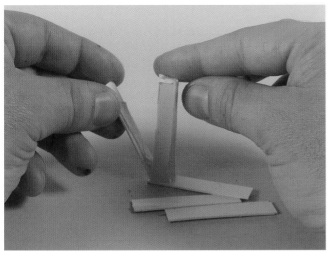

*Once the mixture has dried, remove the
planks and the mould is ready.*

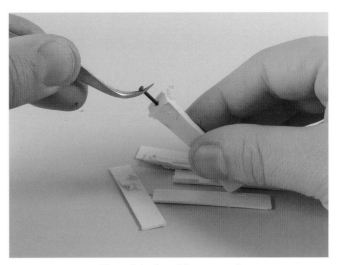

*The original part is removed
from the mould with tweezers.*

• Musing other types of containers

*Simple parts can be cast using containers that held
other products but which meet the required
measurements. In this case, the same part has
been cast in a used Microsol bottle. The process is
exactly the same, beginning by gluing the part to
the bottle base.*

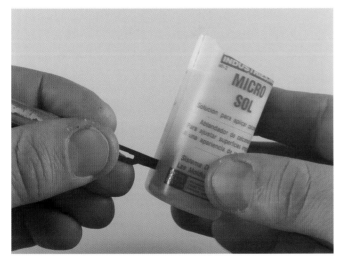

*Once the silicone mixture has been prepared it is poured into
the bottle in the same way as explained earlier. Once the
mould has cured, the container is cut to remove the mould and
the original part.*

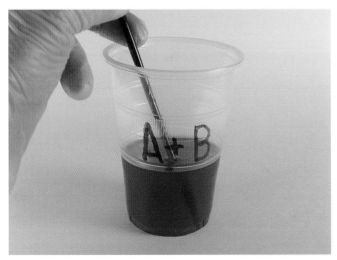

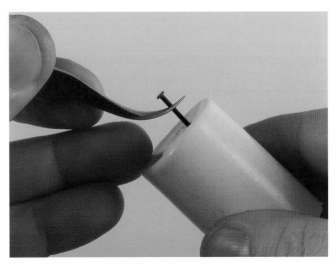

● *Resin*

There are two products, A: resin and B: catalyser. The manufacturer's instructions state that they should be mixed 50:50. To carry out this process, use disposable, transparent plastic glasses that permit for correct measures.

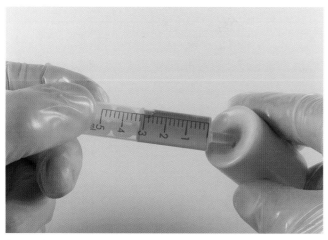

Both products, A and B, are poured into the glass. Protective gloves should be used for handling these products.

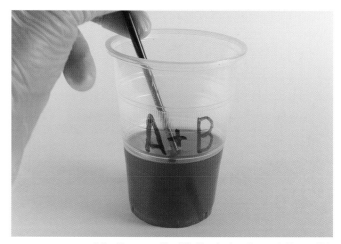

Mix them well with the help of a rod. From this moment, there is just 3 minutes before the resin begins to cure. The mixture will heat up during the curing process due to polymerization.

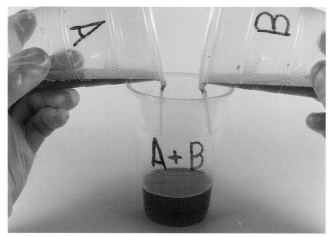

The resin is injected into the mould in an increasing, but careful manner.

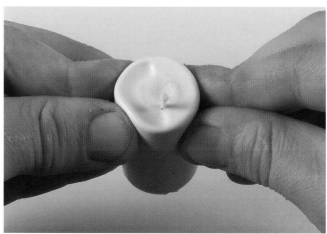

Once resin has totally cured (around 30 minutes), it is time to remove the casting. All that is needed at this point is to remove the part from the mould, exerting a slight finger pressure to it.

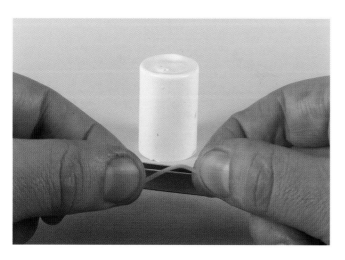

If the part is removed before 30 minutes elapses, it is still possible to shape or bend it to some extent. On the other hand, the casting can be left to 'rests' in the mould for hours to insure maximum hardness.

Here can be seen the final result with the orange ventilation pipe in the centre.
The mould was prepared with the use of a scale bolt and using the method explained above.

27.5 How to make more complex moulds?

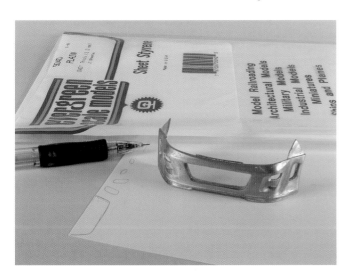

As with the earlier cases, a purpose built container should be constructed to hold the mould. In this case, the part is a front spoiler for a Ford Focus WRC. As can be seen in the photos, some areas should be hollow. To achieve this, these areas should be covered with specially made, very thin plastic patterns that enable us to remove the excess resin (same thickness as the plastic patterns) from the hollows once the casting has been removed.

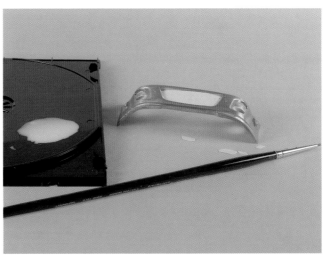

Once the patterns have been trimmed, they are then glued with water-diluted white glue. The seams are sealed with this too.

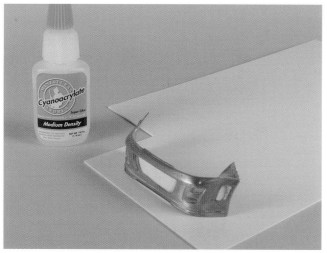

Look for suitable areas on the part to glue it to the base, not forgetting that these particular point will also be the feeder too and that parts will later have to be removed from the mould in the easiest possible way. For this reason, the feeder should not be smaller than the whole part, unless removal became exceedingly difficult or the mould becomes cut, which, in the case of especially intricate parts, is unavoidable.

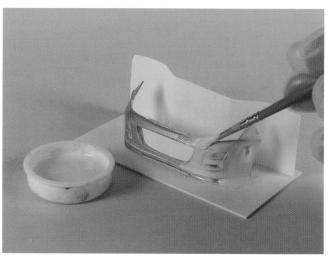

When working with relatively large parts, there is some risk of bubbles sticking to the part that might produce holes in the final casting. A good trick in avoiding this problem is to paint the part with some already prepared silicone and let it cure completely.

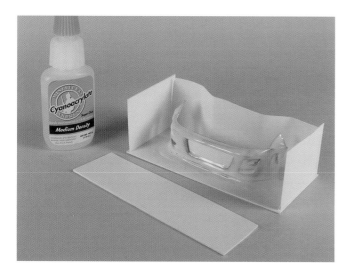

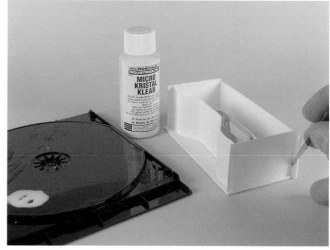

Making the container as already explained.

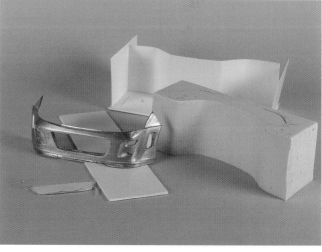

The new silicone mixture is prepared, this time to fill the whole container.
This new one cured perfectly without any bubbles.

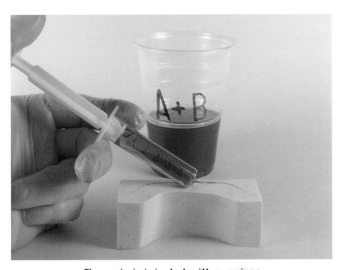

*The resin is injected with a syringe
at reach point in the mould.*

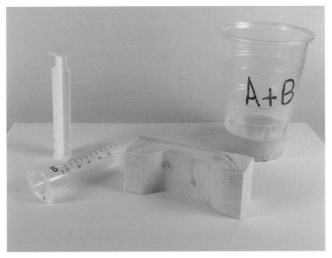

*How resin looks when completely cured. The syringe can be
retained for further use by simply dismantling it after the
casting operation has finished.*

The mould is detached from the part and removed.

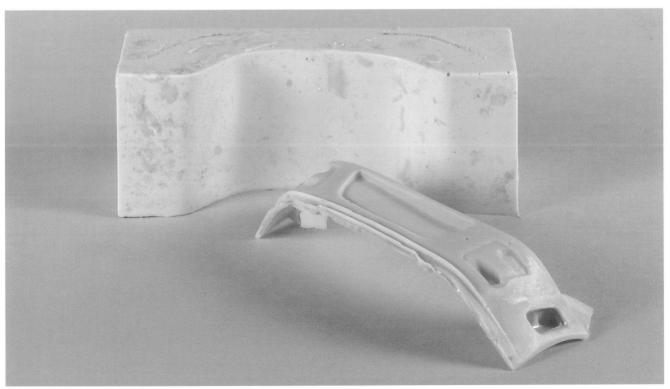

Final look of the completed part. All that remains is remove the resin from the hollows and eliminate any possible flaws.

28. MISCELLANEOUS

Some further interesting points, not looked in previous sections, are dealt with here.

28.1 How to build a rear diffuser?

Some parts supplied with the kit are so over-scale that it is better to think in terms of scratch-building another rather than trying to get them down to a proper size.

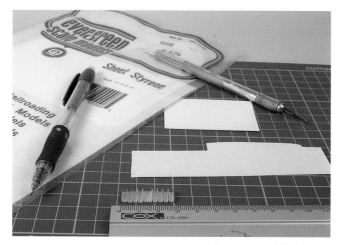

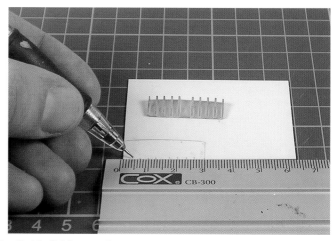

On a piece of Plasticard of suitable thickness, draw the part with its correctly scaled measurements.

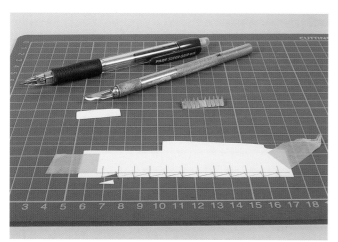

Cut the triangles.

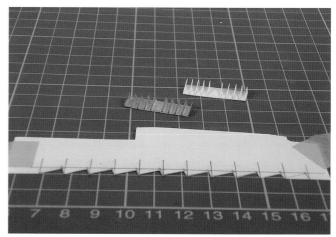

Once the triangles have been glued together, the resulting part can be compared with the original. Note how different the thickness is.

28.2 How to create a shaped logo?

The whole logo is painted
with a background colour,

The relief is sandpapered.
The background remains untouched.

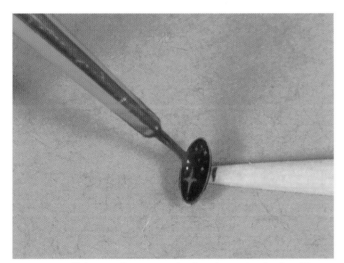

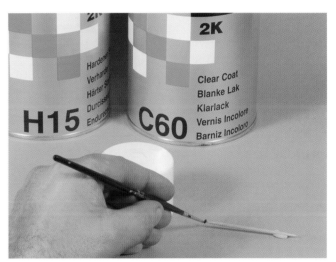

Using car lacquer and a brush, apply plenty of lacquer onto the part. Doing it this way, and after allowing it
to dry for a few days, the result is a shaped -not flat- part. This process can also be done with a decal.
All that is required is to prepare a base onto which decal will be later applied.

28.3 *How to paint clear tubing?*

This technique can be used to simulate liquids inside clear tubing.

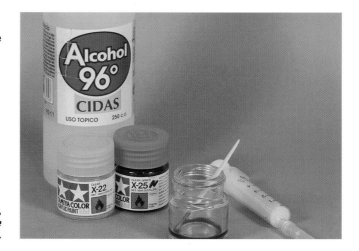

Transparent colours, diluted with alcohol, are injected inside the tube using a syringe fitted with a very fine needle.

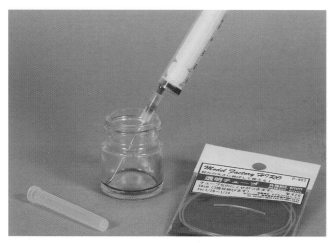

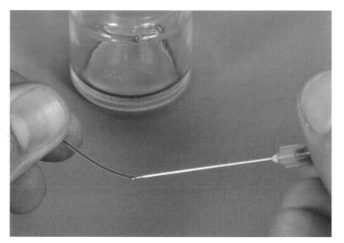

28.4 How to make springs?

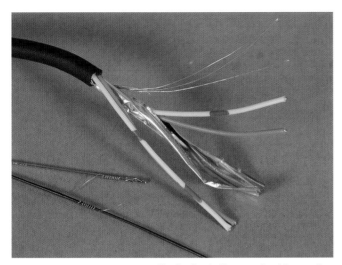 

First, check the required inner diameter of the spring. Then, use electrical wire rolled around a suitable piece of tubing or other round object.

28.5 How to simulate dirt?

In this modelling speciality, be very careful with when applying dirt effects because, if overdone, it could appear that an underlying flaw is being covered up. Some racing car or motorcycle models can be beautifully enhanced using these effects, as is the case of rally or antique cars.

Mixtures of different colours can be prepared until the correct shade is achieved. The mixture, just slightly diluted, is then airbrushed at low air pressure but not before making some tests on a piece of paper. The aim is to spray irregular paint specks to simulate dust and splashes.
Pigments, like those beloved by makers of military models, can also be added but just to specific points.

28.6 How to paint exhaust silencer interiors?

Sometimes a brush will not reach the interior of exhaust pipes, resulting in an unrealistic finish.

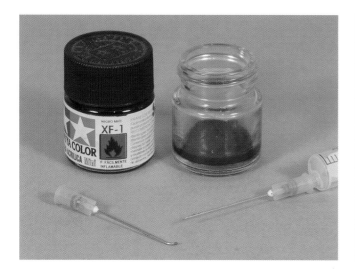

*Using a syringe and, as with the interiors, diluted
paint is applied, in this instance, flat black.*

28.7 How to paint lined up pieces?

*Using a sandwich board or cork base. prepare a guide line with
pins all around parts. Once perfectly lined up, they can be
removed and glued.*

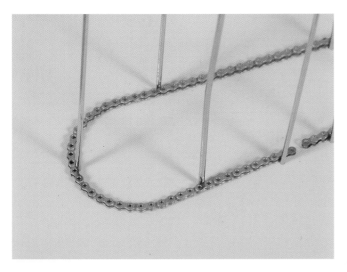 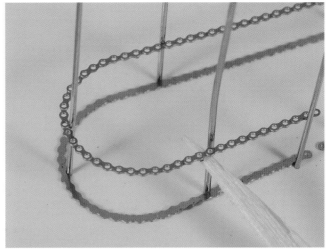

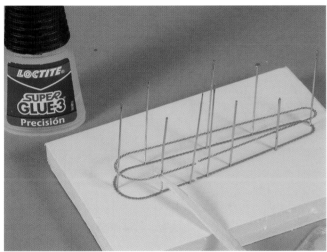 

28.8 How to paint an engine drive chain?

The part is painted in the same colour as the sprocket.

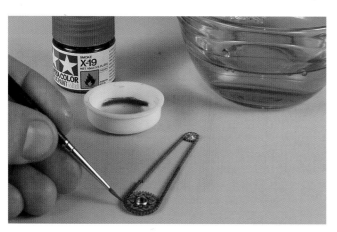

A piece of adhesive masking is prepared that will fit the sprocket's inner diameter. Finally, the chain plates and rollers are painted in another colour.

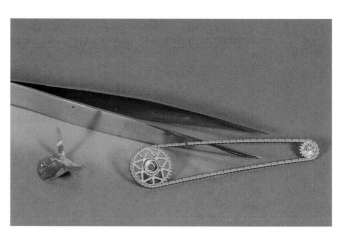

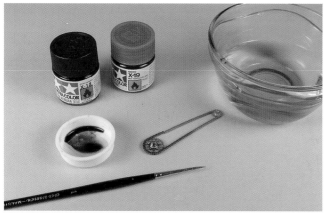

The sprocket and chain are given a wash with a mixture of highly diluted smoke and black.

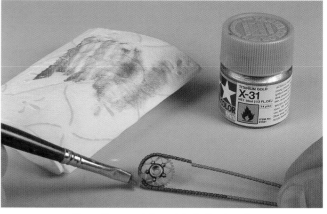

Once the wash has dried, dry brush the chain with a lighter colour than the base.

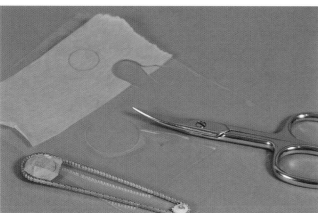

Further washes with highly diluted smoke render an oily effect.

28.9 How to improve the suspension?

Quite a number of original parts can be improved by simply using everyday items such as glasses, small bolts, rods, small nuts, ball pen springs, and so on.

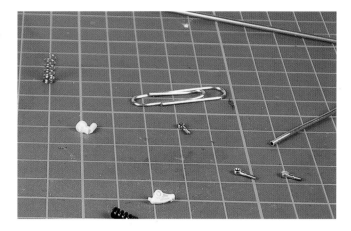

An assortment of different materials.

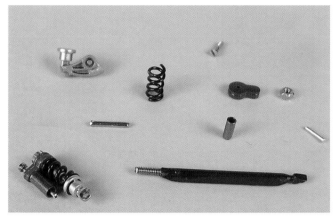

All components are painted separately.

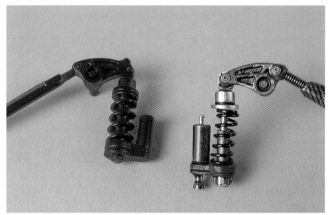

The difference between the original and the improved part is very noticeable.

28.10 How to improve a motorcycle chain guide?

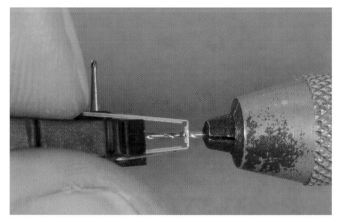

A 0´5 mm drill is used on the box section swing arm. Then a rod or spare bit is fitted. Finally, a nut can also be added to the rod end.

28.11 How to remove dust from models?

Needless to say, completed models should reside in a hermetically sealed showcase. Notwithstanding, some dust may be picked when carrying them to competitions, magazines, photographic sessions or other events. The best way to remove dust is to blow it off with the airbrush.

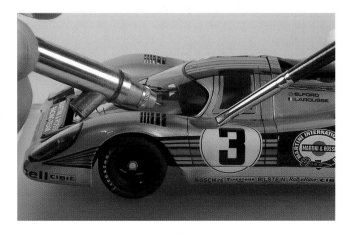

By using a soft brush and low pressure air, dust specks and fuzz are cleaned off.

●GALLERY
OF MODELS USED
IN THIS BOOK

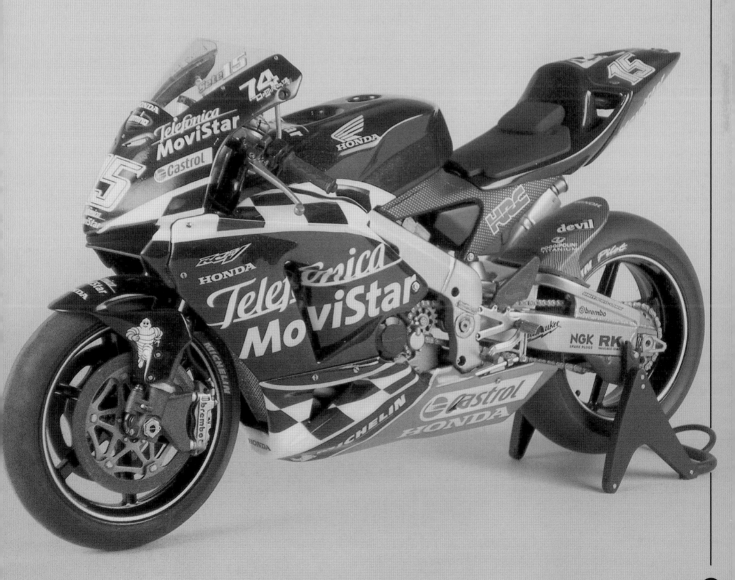

SUBARU IMPREZA WRC
2005 MONTE CARLO RALLY
1/24

TOYOTA GT ONE
LE MANS 1999
1/24

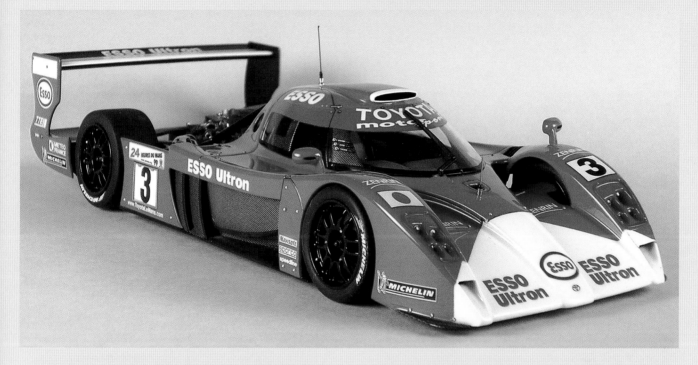

YAMAHA R1 50TH ANNIVERSARY USA
1/12

FERRARI 550 MARANELLO
LE MANS SERIES
1/43

ASTON MARTIN CBR9
1/24

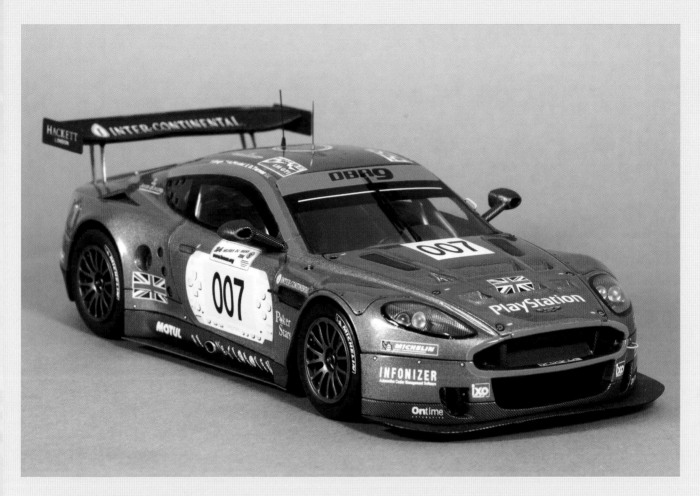

McLAREN MP 4/8
1/43

PERSONAL GALLERY

FERRARI SHARKNOSE
1/20

HONDA RC211V CAMEL TEAM
1/12

FERRARI 550 MARANELLO
1/43

PORSCHE 917K
1/24

PEUGEOT 307 WRC
1/24

CORVETTE GRAND SPORT
1/24

DUCATI DESMOSEDICE GP
1/12

LEXUS SC430
1/24

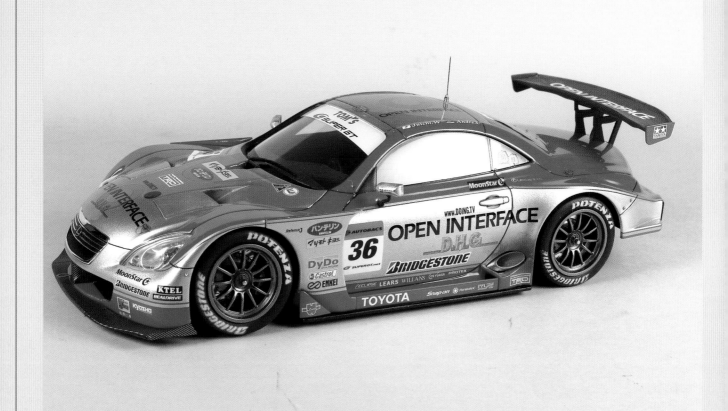

HONDA RC211V TELEFÓNICA MOVISTAR
1/12

FERRARI 550 MARANELLO
1/43

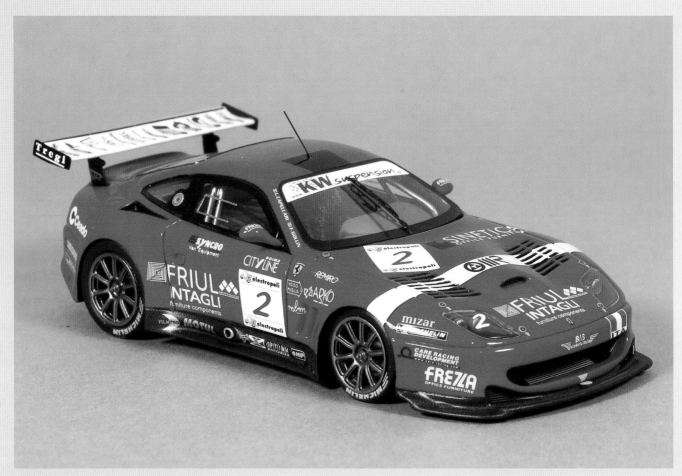

TYRRELL 001
1/12

HONDA RC211V FORTUNA TEAM
1/12

FERRRARI ENZO
1/24

SUZUKI HAYABUSA YOSIMURA
1/12

MERCEDES CLK DTM
1/24

PEUGEOT 206 WRC
1/24

RENAULT R24
1/20

SUZUKI HAYABUSA 1300
1/12

MCLAREN MP4/5
1/43

KAWASAKI ZXRR
1/12